FORCES OF NATURE
FORGING THE CHARACTER OF WINNERS

by LINKED IN AND TOWN HALL ACHIEVER OF THE YEAR
EY NOMINEE ENTREPRENEUR OF THE YEAR
GRAND HOMAGE LYS DIVERSITY
WORLD TOP100 DOCTORS

Dr. BAK NGUYEN, DMD

TO ALL THOSE WONDERING HOW TO FACE THE CHALLENGES
OF LIFELIKE THE HEROES FACED THE DEMONS,
THE ANGELS AND THE GODS

by Dr. BAK NGUYEN

Copyright © 2018 Dr BAK NGUYEN

All rights reserved.

ISBN: 978-1-989536-63-6

Published by: Dr. BAK PUBLISHING COMPANY
Dr.BAK 0015

ABOUT THE AUTHOR

From Canada, **Dr. BAK NGUYEN**, Nominee Ernst and Young Entrepreneur of the year, Grand Homage Lys DIVERSITY, LinkedIn & TownHall Achiever of the year and TOP 100 Doctors 2021. Dr Bak is a cosmetic dentist, CEO and founder of Mdex & Co. His company is revolutionizing the dental field. Speaker and motivator, he wrote 72 books over 36 months accumulating many world records (to be officialized). His books are covering:

- **ENTREPRENEURSHIP**
- **LEADERSHIP**
- **QUEST OF IDENTITY**
- **DENTISTRY AND MEDICINE**
- **PARENTING**
- **CHILDREN BOOKS**
- **PHILOSOPHY**

In 2003, he founded Mdex, a dental company upon which in 2018, he launched the most ambitious private endeavour to reform the dental industry, Canada wide. Philosopher, he has close to his heart the quest of happiness of the people surrounding him, patients and colleagues alike. In 2020, he launched an International collaborative initiative named **THE ALPHAS** to share knowledge and for Entrepreneurs and Doctors to thrive through the Greatest Pandemic and Economic depression of our time.

In 2016, he co-found with Tranie Vo, Emotive World Incorporated, a tech research company to use technology to empower happiness and sharing. U.A.X. the ultimate audio experience is the landmark project on which the team is advancing, utilizing the technics of the movie industry and the advancement in ARTIFICIAL INTELLIGENCE to save the book industry and to upgrade the continuing education space.

These projects have allowed Dr Nguyen to attract interests from the international and diplomatic community and he is now the center of a global discussion in the wellbeing and the future of the health profession. It is in that matter that he shares his thoughts and encourages the health community to share their own stories.

> "It's not worth it go through it alone! Together, we stand, alone, we fall."

Motivational speaker and serial entrepreneur, philosopher and author, from his own words, Dr Nguyen describes himself as a dentist by circumstances, an entrepreneur by nature and a communicator by passion.

He also holds recognitions from the Canadian Parliament and the Canadian Senate.

FORCES OF NATURE
FORGING THE CHARACTER OF WINNERS

by Dr. BAK NGUYEN

INTRODUCTION
by Dr. BAK NGUYEN

CHAPTER 1
INERTIA
by Dr. BAK NGUYEN

CHAPTER 2
MYOPIA
by Dr. BAK NGUYEN

CHAPTER 3
TIME
by Dr. BAK NGUYEN

CHAPTER 4
TRUTH
by Dr. BAK NGUYEN

CHAPTER 5
TWO FACES
by Dr. BAK NGUYEN

CHAPTER 6
EMOTIONS
by Dr. BAK NGUYEN

CHAPTER 7
EXPECTATIONS
by Dr. BAK NGUYEN

CHAPTER 8
ABUNDANCE
by Dr. BAK NGUYEN

CONCLUSION
LIFE, DEATH
by Dr. BAK NGUYEN

INTRODUCTION

"WHAT WAS ONCE INTIMIDATING, IS NOW DÉJÀ VU."

DR. BAK NGUYEN

15 months minus 9 days ago, I started a crazy journey sharing my thoughts, writing books. Today I am about to achieve my own goal, to write 15 books within 15 months.

Literally hours after the completion of the last one, **LEVERAGE**, I am starting my 15th opus. I have to tell you that up to a few hours ago, I wasn't sure what to write, neither if I can finish this month with a win. 15 books written within 15 months will be my mark in the World Guinness Record!

> "INTIMIDATION CAN ONLY OCCUR WHEN YOU STOP AND STARE IT IN THE EYES. KEEP MOVING AND IT WILL BE JUST A DOT IN TIME."
> Dr. BAK NGUYEN

As I sat down that morning, I didn't know how to finish the month and my challenge. How about stripping down completely? Yes, this would be my 15 books within 15 months, why not finish with a big bang? Why not talk about all my greatest challenges and what I learnt from them.

The idea is surely a great one, but isn't that dangerous to share in a single book most of my mistakes and weaknesses? Won't that give away the blueprint to defeat me in the future?

To that, a crazy thought smiled at me, and made me realize that my own evolution and speed will prevent that from happening since I will have outgrown all of them. To have the audacity to write about them boldly is the best way to suppress their weight in my mind.

For the last 15 months, I learnt to open up and to share, honestly but a single bite at a time. Now to have a book comprised of the density of my challenges, surely, it will be a first to me. Actually, if I thought that I was exposing myself before, it was nothing compared to this endeavour. It's like making a movie only with action sequences… even the action itself might lose some of its value.

This book promises to strip me down naked to the bones. But why not? I love the confidence! I just finished a book about communication, imagine the narrative I am drafting with a book comprised of my biggest challenges?

On the upside, this book will write itself up since I'll be writing from memory instead of from projection. A great and needed break since I have signed 5 books within the last 3 months to reach my goal.

The first title that came to my mind was **CHALLENGER**. I love the directness of the title and what it represents. But out of respect to the tragic end of the space shuttle and its crew, I withdrew myself from using that title.

I am a challenger, but what challenges me? The *Forces of Nature*, all of them, one after the next. If I am lucky, I will only face them one at a time. They are playing with me, pushing me, sometimes even laughing at me. But if I keep my spirit up, if I can face the *Forces of Nature* and still keep my head high, they are training me into one of them.

The secret here is not to be shy, intimidated nor arrogant. I am not provoking the fights, the trials nor the tests, I am simply walking my path. Whatever I face, I must get through and if I am still alive on the other side, I will have grown from the encounter. Eventually, even the *Forces of Nature* will gain respect from my tenacity... I hope.

> "EVENTUALLY, WHAT WAS ONCE INTIMIDATING, IS NOW DÉJÀ VU."
> Dr. BAK NGUYEN

I read once: "It never gets easier, we are only getting stronger!" Sure thing! I keep my eyes on the prize and really, nothing is really hard if you tackle the problem a bit at a time, feeding on your last win, as small as it is, and gaining both *momentum* and confidence from that victory. Then, don't stop, take advantage of the *momentum* to go straight to the next challenge!

It's either it or me? That's what I am telling myself every single time. Actually, that was how I started. Today with more wisdom and experience, I am looking for ways to avoid the confrontation first. I am lazy, remember? I will try all the other alternatives first before charging head down! But it I must, I will charge, it is either it or me!

What an improvement in maturity you will say! Not exactly. Can you imagine that this exact maturity and restraint over myself has also become a weakness perceived by the smaller minds? This trait of personality has become a liability and a challenge by itself!

> " WE OFTEN FACE THE CHALLENGES WE DESERVE... "
> Dr. BAK NGUYEN

The smaller minds interpreted that restraint as cowardliness, kindness as stupidity, and the avoidance of a fight as indecision. They don't stand a chance in a face-to-face, I am simply trying to avoid wasting energy and futile casualties. At the end of my day, my positive ledger is still what is judging me, what kind of man am I, if I unleash at all those coming at me...

> " CONTROL IS ONE OF THE GREATEST OF POWER.
> POWER OVER ONESELF."
> Dr. BAK NGUYEN

From that, a new challenge emerged: the challenge to remain in control and unchanged by the event. The strength and determination to keep what I deem good and kind in my heart to simply ignore those who are trying to break or knock me down.

> "YOU WILL NEVER ERASE THAT SMILE ON MY FACE NOR THE LIGHT OF JOY AND HOPE IN MY HEART."
> Dr. BAK NGUYEN

What an irony? But wait, if I was trained by the *Forces of Nature* to grow and now I am challenged by my own personality traits, does that mean that I have become a *Force of Nature* myself? I will let you be the judge of that.

I will simply take the opportunity to reflect on my steps and to make sense of everything. The exercise I need, the cleaning up I crave, the label, I do not care. Not anymore.

Welcome to my 15th opus: **FORCES OF NATURE**, forging the character of winners. As I was in a rush against TIME to write this book within a little more than a week, I became insecure. I was enthusiast to start the cover, the title, the introduction, and the first chapter. The writing was always flawless and smooth but I didn't feel anything writing them. I panicked!

Have I lost my touch? It is simply impossible to write about my past challenges and to not feel anything! Was it fatigue or the fact that I was at the end of the road of my career as a writer?

To complicate things, I could not back down anymore since I posted on my LinkedIn and other social networks profile that I was entering the last book, **FORCES OF NATURE**, of my journey to reach 15 books written within 15 months.

So I asked my counsellor, Brenda Garcia, who is also known as my conscience to give me some feedback. Time is so short, if I need to readjust, it has to be in a matter of hours, not days! She went through the introduction and the first chapters and was… perplexed. She read most of my writing until now and to her, I was starting to repeat myself.

I needed to find an original twist to this book to not be a burden by doing just another book telling the same story one more time. After 14 books, I can be a little confused about what I already said and what I haven't share yet…

I slept on the criticism, a part of me, knowing that it has a truth laying underneath. The next day, I woke up at 7 AM. 7! I was supposed to be up at 5 AM to have the time to write and I am on such a tight schedule! Was that a message that my body was sending too?

I refused to bow down and spent the next 30 minutes of the morning trying to find a solution to twist the energy and the vibe of the 15th project. Until now, each of my books has a picture with a quote per chapter. How about I twist that entry and use it as leverage? I went online and started producing a "cover" to personalize and to introduce each of the **FORCES OF NATURE** that I had encountered. From *Inertia* to *Emotions* and *lies*, I started to brand them one by one.

That changed the whole perspective of the writing and the promise of the fun coming with it. I sat down with Brenda to test my new theory… it worked, she was now amazed!

This 15th opus, if it is my last book will be an apogee and a bridge. A bridge to what's next to come. I now have 7 days to deliver and I have high hopes!

This is **FORCES OF NATURE**. Welcome to the Alphas.

> ALL MY CHALLENGES
> WERE THE BIGGEST
> AS I FACED THEM
> AND VAGUE SOUVENIRS
> AS I MOVED ON
>
> Dr. BAK NGUYEN

CHAPTER 1 - INERTIA

"INERTIA WAS NOT TO STAND STILL BUT TO FIND THE STRENGTH TO DEAL WITH MULTIPLE OPPOSITES AND TO KEEP BALANCE."

DR. BAK NGUYEN

The first and foremost *Force of Nature* that I had to face all my life, as an individual and an entrepreneur was *Inertia*. Not mine, but other's tendency and latency to stand still or to wait for the perfect conditions.

You have no idea of how hard it is to try to fit in and to convince yourself that it is the right thing to do: to slow down, to ignore your nature, your call, your strength and to channel most of your vital energy just to keep control over yourself.

As an individual, it was hard, almost cruel, but it was a great character forger. I am fast, in most things, fast to learn, fast to move, fast to get back up. Within my *"time in Conformity"*, I had to learn to stay in line and to exchange with my peers. The training gave me depth.

That's how I kept everyone happy: on the surface, I was tuning down, dimming most of my energies to stand still and not to disturb. I kept a low profile of what people labelled as arrogance and attention deficit problems.

I dove in instead, diving into myself to understand the feelings and their mechanisms. As I got better and better at diving into my soul, I realized that I could also rise and fly since the dimensions were infinite, at least from the perspective of a child.

I learnt to fly within my mind, discovering my *wings of creativity*. The only *still* that remains is when I forgot myself and started sharing my views with the outside world.

I was *"special"* but not in a good way since I was making most people feel uncomfortable with ideas they were not familiar with. The silly fact is that I was often answering one of their problems... but they were always looking for the answers they got on papers or better, written in stone.

My inability to keep quiet while I was trying to help and to contribute often got the best of me. Respect! That word slapped me in the face at every single time.

> **"AS A SOCIETY, WE RESPECT MORE AUTHORITY THAN EFFICIENCY."**
> Dr. BAK NGUYEN

With that kind of comment, arrogance became my second name. If you put everything in perspective, I was born Canadian, inside of an immigrant family where my parents were fighting to provide for their kids while looking for their place in a new society...

I soon learnt a precious lesson: to choose my battles. For a quick learner, it surely took me years to completely master myself, and to choose the right battles, those I really have to win.

#1 Choose your battle

Today, *Creativity* is one of my best skills and attribute in life. Creativity allows me to redefine the limits and the boundaries, to look for new resources and new ways to tackle almost all the challenges that I face. If it wasn't for my forced exiled since childhood, I might not have developed my mental wings as powerfully. That's how I see it today, gratefully.

> " GRACE AND GRATITUDE ARE THE BEST AND MY ONLY WAYS TO LOOK AT THE PAST AND TO KEEP SOMETHING GOOD FROM IT."
> Dr. BAK NGUYEN

The **ANGEL OF LIFE**. If Life was a female entity, Life would be my wife and lover. Life has been good and great to me, wrapping me with care and love and, each time, allowing me a chance to heal and to grow stronger from each trial.

Thanks to love, I succeeded to keep a positive spirit throughout most of the ups and downs. Thanks to the love of Life, the angel, I have forged the precious shield of Gratitude to face adversity and darkness.

Since I can create and redraft the future, it is not worth it to try so hard to ignore and to erase the past. I found a better way, I can edit my past, keeping the best angles, forcing myself to find the good in people and in the events, and thanking them for their contributions.

I was lucky enough to have coped positively with most of my challenges, trials, and deceptions. My life isn't perfect, but I leveraged the events to reach the person that I am today, and I am still not broken! I am a source of inspiration for many. That's who I am and what I choose to keep from the past, the people helping me to reach myself fully.

Yesterday I got video interviewed by a group of undergrad students for their entrepreneurship class in business school. I did not get prepared in advance and gave myself freely to answer all of their questions. From their enthusiasm, I couldn't ignore the fact that despite the pain and sweat, the ignorance and rejection, I was pretty well treated, if not by all people, by Life itself.

And then, the right people showed up. I remember that they asked me the same question: how did I accept my different nature as an entrepreneur and how did get it accepted by the others? By finding worth!

You see, I was always stuck between what my parents and teachers told me that I was, and should do, and what I felt right doing. So I discovered, playing in both fields. Eventually, I did, and became both!

The person society wanted me to become, a logical, structured and disciplined individual, reliable and trustworthy, that doctor my parents wished and worked all their life for. To honour both their love and sacrifices, I became a respected and accomplished doctor in dentistry.

Thanks to the love from Life, I also grew into the artist and the human ambassador that I always felt inside. Actually, my sensitivity and kindness were what made me a successful dentist in the first place: I care about the person, not the teeth! Guess what? That was music to my patients' ears!

Today, I have developed both sides of my brains, the left, and the right, equally. If it wasn't from my *"time in Conformity"*, I might have never grown as powerful and complete. I am not saying that I am perfect, I guess what I am saying here, is that I am grateful to have found the path to my destiny not having to reject and to challenge society to find my voice.

> "I AM NOT PERFECT, THEY ARE NOT PERFECT. LET'S LEAVE IT AT THAT."
> Dr. BAK NGUYEN

That last line is the key to navigate successfully through the troubled waters as I felt alone, in the middle of an ocean of unknown with nothing to reference to. They are entitled to their opinions, so am I. But I got wiser: if they do not know my opinion, I can easily avoid a fight which will lead to nothing but wounded pride.

So the burden of their judgments on me became lesser and lesser. This is a hard lesson learnt. The pain is mainly coming from the fact that it is a very slow lesson to learn, at least for me...

> "I STOP LETTING PEOPLE JUDGE ME WITH THEIR OPINIONS, EVEN WITH LOVE, THEY ALL HAVE THEIR BOUNDARIES."
> Dr. BAK NGUYEN

I was raised with values and honour. Those I hold dear to my heart. Those values have passed the test of time, from my own choices and freedom. Even if I have to recover from suffering and injustices, it does not mean that I had to scar bitter. On the contrary, I healed with happiness and the conviction that the best is ahead since I am now in control, in better control of myself, and in harmony with nature.

So I learnt to surf and to thrive over the *forces of Inertia*, choosing my battle and making the best of the *"time in Conformity"*. Now that I am out, I leave Inertia where it belongs, in the past, with respect and gratitude, but it stays in the past.

Later on in life, as I was still doing my *"time"*, and I got bored from flying within my creativity and soul, I started to expand my horizons, to dive into others. I know, it doesn't sound great, but trust me, it is nothing invasive or disrespectful, it is called **empathy**.

Knowing my own feeling and the mechanisms, I started observing those surrounding me and often noticed that what they were saying and how they act and move were often in contradiction. I felt their pain.

As I was curious, I tried to figure out how and why they were that way, why, and what they were feeling. Feelings, and logic, that's how I came to understand them for what there were. I am not judging, I feel.

And as I feel, my nature often pushes me to offer comfort and solutions. That's how I became respected and loved, more and more. From an arrogant, I was now kind and good. The good doctor.

Trust me, it wasn't always easy to open up and to offer a kind hand. Time and time again, people will bite you as soon as they got what they need. But it is not about you, it's about them.

With empathy, I can now see it coming and protect myself. To protect myself, not to close myself down because that would mean a defeat in my personal evolution. To keep evolving, **openness** is the only way to grow. Closing down might speed up the process in the short term until we run out of fuel. To move forward, one needs to replenish and to keep accelerating.

> "ONE NEEDS TO REPLENISH WITHOUT SLOWING DOWN."
> Dr. BAK NGUYEN

Empathy was my way to connect with people. I didn't have that ability from birth. I had to develop it as I did my *"time in Conformity"*. Empathy allowed me to feel and to understand the people, any and everyone I encountered.

Not completely but enough to predict their behaviours and to act accordingly. From empathy, my communication skills got a major upgrade. Now I know who I am talking to. With the right words and the right motivation, I can get most people to join my views, freely and joyfully.

How did I do that? I feel their pain and desire. Often, I am offering them a genuine solution, an alternative to their reality. Even if they might reject it at first, they will eventually come around. My training as a doctor helped my personal evolution on the matter, to always put the interests of my patients first.

That has become second nature, to always fight my worth serving the other. By putting their interests at the centre of my attention, our connection is always genuine and often fruitful as both parties know what they are looking for.

Empathy and communication, but there is more. With much *"time"* spent in Conformity, I have also learnt to love my peers, even those who hated me and were throwing rocks at me. Love might be a strong word but hate was simply a too exhausting way to grow from. There are **Love**, **Hate**, and **Ignorance**.

> " I TRY TO LOVE FIRST AND IF THAT IS NOT WORKING, THEN, I IGNORE."
> Dr. BAK NGUYEN

That's my way, my lazy way to go through life. And the love I have developed, allowed me to mature into a leader, a real leader, one that understands the nuance and the consequences of each of his actions, the good and the bad.

I bear today the title of *Industries Disruptor*, I intend to change the world for the better, but each time, I am deeply aware of the collateral damages. I create, I do not destroy, but every time I create something new, I am also replacing something old.

Even broken, that system had people and an ecosystem revolving around it. With empathy and love, I hold myself accountable and force myself to be aware of the consequences. Doing so, I will try to avoid as many collaterals as possible. That's how I try to keep a positive ledger at the end of each day.

The world is not black and white, and I have learnt to appreciate all the nuances of grey. I am one of these depths in nuance and I am grateful to have the chance to express myself, freely. From *Inertia* and my *time in Conformity*, I grew stronger and wiser, balanced and aware of both faces of each situation.

> "INERTIA WAS NOT TO STAND STILL BUT TO FIND THE STRENGTH TO DEAL WITH MULTIPLE OPPOSITES AND TO KEEP BALANCE."
> Dr. BAK NGUYEN

To get back at my interview yesterday, the last question the students asked me was: What advice would I give to my younger self if I had the chance. Within 30 seconds of reflection, I was surprised by my own answer. I will just keep going my way.

Now that I've found my way and my mission in life, everything, bad and good that happened to me lead me to where and who I am today. I won't do anything to jeopardize that. I am the sum of all my experiences and choices. Change once, and I am not the same anymore. For that reason, I reinforce my beliefs in gratitude.

> "THE PAST GOT ME THE POTENTIAL TO WRITE THE FUTURE."
> Dr. BAK NGUYEN

For that reason, I treasure my past, but I am not living in it nor spending too much time thinking about it. I move forward with lightness and an open heart, embracing the new day welcoming me. Nature has accepted me and its Forces are training me as one of their own.

This is **FORCES OF NATURE**. Welcome to the Alphas.

> ALL MY CHALLENGES
> WERE THE BIGGEST
> AS I FACED THEM
> AND VAGUE SOUVENIRS
> AS I MOVED ON
> Dr. BAK NGUYEN

CHAPTER 2 - MYOPIA

"TO BEAT MYOPIA, GO FAST! YOU'LL BE AMAZED HOW FAR YOU CAN GO."

DR. BAK NGUYEN

After *Inertia*, *Myopia* was the next Force of Nature that I had to battle. It is something to be in movement, but to have your sight constantly clouded by ignorance and fear is surely frustrating. The difficulty battling *Myopia* is that it is subtle and discreet, always hiding itself behind the presence of others. There is always an excuse to justify the wait and the delay.

How to move forward and to keep on track when nothing is sure to even exist? The favourite minions of *Myopia* are *Doubt*, *Fear*, *Laziness*, and *Ignorance*. Oh, there are many more, actually, everything *Myopia* can throw at us, it will, and never, you might even see its face. It is a master of hiding its presence.

The secret power of *Myopia* is not just what it is throwing at us, its secret power is that it doesn't even need to aim right. *Myopia*, remember! From Doubt and Fear, if we finally managed to escape the direct attempt, like a *dirty bomb*, they still explode and affect all of those surrounding us.

The effect will be the same: smoke, dirt, and obstruction of the line of sight. With a short sight, the truth is changing colour and textures... To come back from this illusion is possible but often frustrating and very time-consuming.

> "THE GOAL OF MYOPIA IS TO SLOW US DOWN,
> STOP US OR MAKE US GOING IN ROUND CIRCLES."
> Dr. BAK NGUYEN

In my case, *Myopia* started as *Ignorance* and *Laziness*. Those two were enough to keep me from reaching the horizon and discovering a clear line of sight. With time, the accumulation of knowledge took care of *Ignorance*. And *Laziness*? He still hangs around every day. But he can't, by himself, obstruct the horizon, once one knows the way.

I am lazy. Not because I do not move forward, but because I will always choose the quickest way to get out of a given task. I do not care about the protocol nor the journey, I care about the fun, the efficiency, and particularly, the result.

When I first started an independent movie back at school, I was facing the pure unknown. I never did anything like this before and no one around me knew better. It wasn't *Myopia*, it was total darkness. I did it to escape the boredom of dental school. The daily beacon of hope was the fun we had on stage as the lights went up and the cameras were rolling.

I do not have to tell you how crazy the idea was and how people were expecting us to fail miserably. But the funny thing is, it was so crazy that most people were just smiling and encouraging! You know, just to be kind enough to not crush the hope of a young dreamer. I realized what they were really thinking the day I delivered a final product. From the look in their eyes, I understood the hypocrisy and the mesmerizing!

In general, people believe in the past and in what they know. It's a way to say that they are trap within what is and what was. To believe in the future, a future different from yesterday is not a natural ability given to most people. To be the first to do something is always a sure way to stand alone on the balance of trust. When it is the first time that you are doing something, you often face the same odds and trials!

"THEY WERE ALL BETTING AGAINST ME!"
Dr. BAK NGUYEN

Standing alone against *Myopia* taught me a precious lesson: where ever people were betting, I now became a reason for them to pick a side! I started to matter! This is how I grew immune from *Myopia* and its effects on my surroundings. Sure, from time to time, it can be frustrating to always go back and to reassure the team... There is an old African saying that everyone has heard: "Alone you go fast, together, we go far."

> **"TO BEAT MYOPIA, GO FAST! YOU'LL BE AMAZED HOW FAR YOU CAN GET."**
> Dr. BAK NGUYEN

Feed from your wins, as small as they are, it will help you gain confidence and insight. When the light is not coming through the thickness of the forest or the darkness of the fog, the light must come from inside… for a little while.

The problem with fuelling from the inside hope for too long is that eventually, it will run out. Even worst, to survive solely from our internal strengths, we will develop a tunnel vision, habits, and filters that will keep us with a limited and **fixed focus**. If that crystallized, we will never be able to see anything else, even when facing a clear horizon. Fighting *Myopia*, we will have embraced it, thinking that we've won!

> **"FLEXIBILITY OF THE MIND, IT IS THE STRONGEST ABILITY."**
> Dr. BAK NGUYEN

Preconceived ideas, fix rules and fix sciences, arrogance are all the kinds of tunnel visions that will slowly enslave and handicap our views and keep us in the forest, forever. My *time in Conformity* got me to be docile and to follow.

My initiatives as an entrepreneur and an artist allowed me to break the curse of *Myopia* since the field, colours and textures were so different. Going from one to the next, I kept my focus flexible, always having to adapt to the field I was on. That preserved my sight for a little while.

It was great but not enough. Eventually, success came and the habits became skills, the reflexes, certainties, and the preconceived ideas, truths. This is how I *"plateau"* and stayed relatively dormant for the next 15 years, changing the world a smile at a time being a dentist. I was successful, I was stable and I had a great life... but I was also dying inside.

It took me a while to notice the rust on my armour and the limited movements I was able to choose from to advance. The movements were specific and designed for my function, to keep the flow stable and smooth.

I was always meeting with the same people or the same kind of people. I was eating every day the same food and feeding on the same dream for years. There was no need and no chance to break the circular rounds.

> "MYOPIA GOT THE BEST OF ME, TRAPPING ME IN MY OWN ARMOUR, MY OWN SUCCESS."
> Dr. BAK NGUYEN

I needed more, I craved for more... until the day I pressed reset, a hard reset. To break a habit is a task hard enough, to break from the habits that brought us success is an almost impossible task! It will take most of our willpower and the complete negligence of our safety systems.

In one word, we are now standing alone, naked and against ourselves. Even the armour we left behind will have taken a life of its own, continuing to repeat the same movements for a while until our essence eventually completed evaporated out of our old skin. That can last for years. This is how powerful *Myopia* can be, trapping a soul into itself!

I escaped *Myopia* attending a speaking event. Actually, I was invited to speak as a panellist at the John Molson School of Business, Concordia University. It is there that I received the title of *Industries Disruptor*. It was my first real experience as a guest speaker.

I enjoyed it, made new friends, and was ready to finally go home. I was ambushed at the door by the producer of the event, Thierry Lindor, a brother and respected friend who insisted that I stayed on for the main speaker. Sure, said my words, but my heart was dying to go home to find some rest.

I went in as a VIP guest, seated in the middle of a front row! I was stuck, I couldn't even leave before the end. For twenty minutes, I was listening talks about how hard life was when we first embraced our dreams... I didn't know the man, but he was a YouTube sensation, I been told.

I have to tell you that I am a doctor and a CEO. I am shaped a little square and I am also a little… snobby. Usually, I learnt from experts and exchanges with bright, if not the brightest minds of industries. To be seated in an auditorium, stuck to listen to the difficulties of a fail movie maker as he was trying to survive, was not very inspiring.

Every time we encounter someone, there are only two possibilities: either we connect and bond, allowing a synergy and the amplification of our respective vibes or we compare to differentiate. In that case, the energy will be ploughing since one will try to "eat" the other.

I tried, I really tried! For twenty painful minutes, I tried to connect with the man. For twenty minutes, I failed to find any shred of compatibility. So I did the only thing left to do, I compared. Then, something magical happened. As I was looking through the dates and the events, he and I shared much in common.

We were both failed movie makers and we were having a hard time finding our rightful places. He served and survived delivering packages, I did, delivering smiles. From every events until lately, I was ahead of him, way ahead! And yet, I am sitting in the room today, listen to the main speaker of the event, him!

He was a big star, a source of inspiration for the new generation. To be honest, people came to the event to hear him speak. I was more a side dish! What did I miss? I suddenly was fortunate to be stuck in the auditorium until the end!

Because at the end of his talk, everything became clear: he and I were both creative geniuses. We can produce and create as our minds and feelings move freely. The difference is that he gave into the freedom. He created what was on his mind and then, made it available on YouTube. And he moved on to the next, and the next. Some succeeded and some failed...

Compare to him, I was so cheap with my own creativity! I was stuck in my training wheels as a doctor and what made my success until then: planning and aiming for home runs and perfection, every single time. If I can not see a victory, a clear and big victory, I will be holding back my play until the perfect conditions present themselves.

"PERFECTION IS A LIE."
Dr. BAK NGUYEN

I should have known better! Up to that point, I've already written 5 books and just received the refusal of my first book by the biggest French publishing companies in the country. It was surely a setback both in momentum and morale.

I grew prudent and I was planning carefully my next move... but my real talent was to write books, not to publish nor to sell them. That's what I learnt that day! I was being cheap with my creativity! Let's write books and put them out there so I can move on to the next and the next. So what if I miss-played one book, I can write a new one within a month!

That's how I won the day against *Myopia*. I promised myself a hard reset, one that will break all the old habits. I started to say YES to all the proposals, or almost. To protect myself, I referred all the financial decisions to my partner and wife, Tranie Vo. But mainly, I opened myself up 360 degrees and promised myself to keep that course of action for at least the next twelve months.

Seven months into the YESMAN challenge and I have accumulated 10 books more than the first 5, 2 are already available on Amazon. I have received two honours, **Achiever of the year by the LinkedIn Award and Town Hall** and a **Nomination for Ernst and Young for Entrepreneur of the Year**! Even the **Guinness Record** is now within reach! By opening up and by forcing myself to stop judging people, I also got a break from judging myself too! That allowed me to move freely, discovering new horizons and connecting with new people!

Myopia gave me an identity and a standing. My reset allowed me to free myself from that shiny armour. What I thought was my most precious achievement was actually my prison. I have never been happier to embrace each day, not knowing how it will end. I am still building from experience and taking full advantage of my skills set but I took back the control.

> "I WALK AND MY SKILLS CLEAR THE WAY.
> NOT WALKING THE WAY THAT MY SKILLS CAN CLEAN."
> Dr. BAK NGUYEN

And what do you know? Walking the new paths, I discovered new skills! For now, *Myopia* has lost its grasp on me. Until I "*plateau*" again, I am free for a little while. I just needed to remind myself to be aware and to stay humble to avoid its traps ahead. And I know, *Myopia* is never too far away…

This is **FORCES OF NATURE**. Welcome to the Alphas.

> ALL MY CHALLENGES
> WERE THE BIGGEST
> AS I FACED THEM
> AND VAGUE SOUVENIRS
> AS I MOVED ON
>
> Dr. BAK NGUYEN

CHAPTER 3 - TIME

"ONCE I KISSED HER LIPS, THE AMBITION WAS ON
AND THAT FIRE IS HARD TO EXTINGUISH."

DR. BAK NGUYEN

Amongst the Forces of Nature, *TIME* was, and still is, one that eluded most of my expectations and understanding. She always succeeds to catch me off guard and strikes when I least expected, making me her bitch.

Not subtle at all, she even finds fun doing so and bragging about it. And then, it was my turn. Having mastered the skill of *speed* and *momentum*, more than once, I shredded her fabric, moving faster and further than logic and gravity allowed.

Every time I came out on top, *TIME* is laying down her guard and is embracing me in her arms as a powerful conqueror and we made love, passionately. Enough with her to extract enough of my essence and to enslave me back again with tight datelines. She is doing so as I am pleasuring at her mercy. She is enslaving me once more with my own will.

TIME is a powerful and desirable lover to someone like me, shuffling from desire to pleasure, from daring to challenge, from enjoyment to insult. *TIME* can be hormonal and bipolar, but as she bites her lips and looks into our eyes, we gave up everything to please her. And then, to prove her wrong. Very distant from the warm love of the *Angel of Life* which I am married to. To sleep with the *Angel of TIME* is a must and also a curse.

From a young age, *speed* was a second nature to me. By moving fast, I kept balance, by moving constantly, I fought

Ignorance, by moving forward, I was running away from boredom. In the beginning, it was about beating the next guy, then, as I grew older, it was about beating the average. Today, it's mainly about beating myself, my own expectations.

TIME was the *Force of Nature* holding my hand gently at the beginning of my journey. She was cheering and clapping her hands after each win, showing support and sharing my pride! After the first kiss, she changed her attitude, completely.

She became demanding, for more, for better. She eventually, only showed up from time to time, making her presence desirable, dependable. I learnt to both hate and love her all at once.

> "ONCE I KISSED HER LIPS, THE AMBITION WAS ON AND THAT FIRE IS HARD TO EXTINGUISH."
> Dr. BAK NGUYEN

Is *TIME* a commodity in life as many believe? Everything in Life is a commodity that can be traded. The problem with trading *TIME* is that it is not constant and its value fluctuates greatly. Sometimes, *TIME* is the kind lover waiting patiently. At other times, she is that *lover bitch* who makes us beg for no reason at all. I've seen both her faces and I have grown dependent on both of them.

If the love of the *Angel of Life* is keeping me kind and sain, the desire for the *Angel of Time* is poking my systems, waking it from both *Inertia* and *Myopia*, always daring me to do more, more, and always faster and bigger.

A year ago, I started writing. My first book was completed within two weeks! That was a great mark! Then, another and another. As I proved myself to the world, the victory and the control I had over my mistress, *TIME*, she endured the bragging for a while and even gave herself to the celebrations, only to get me fooled later on!

Today, I am her bitch, running to try to accomplish my challenges, almost counting the hours. And I will win, just leaving most of my purest emotions on the table.

> "THAT'S HOW SEX WORKS, SOMETIMES YOU'RE ON TOP AND SOME OTHER TIMES, YOU ARE PINNED DOWN. THE PLEASURE IS IN THE MOVEMENT."
> Dr. BAK NGUYEN

If that was as simple, she would have played it fair. But *TIME* is not a kind lover. A month ago, I got robbed. A thief went into my CEO office and stole my laptops and the work on them.

I lost the complete **EAX** projects that I was about to release. **EAX**, Enhanced Audio Experience, a new way to make books accessible to the general audience. We were weeks from the release and boom! I was falling flat on my belly, my face in the mud!

By itself, this is bad. Add to it the multiple launches of the **Mdex Group**, my company, and the financial stress coming with each of the launches, and you have a more accurate portrait of the situation. The circumstances were strangely similar to what happened before the release of my first movie, **QUESTION DE PERCEPTION**, nearly 20 years ago.

That was a psychological anchor that nearly cost me my sanity and health. The immediate danger here was to run out of time. But the real danger was for me to be projected back in time and to be swallowed by an old anchor.

The consequences could be disastrous if I lose my morale and faith now. The whole playbook will come crumbling down since I am the glue holding most of the pieces together. I was well aware of the dangers and of what was really at stake.

To fuck with *TIME* once more was my only way out! As she was playing with me, I surprised her from the back and took her from behind, without any pleasure.

I speeded up my already frenetic pace of production. I went into *overdrive mode*, feeding my momentum with my own emotions. *Happiness* and *hope* were the first victims of the grinding. I opened more and more projects.

There were piling up as a mountain on my shoulders and I knew, I will have to answer for each of them. If I can keep up that pace for more than a month, I knew that it will become my new baseline and that I will have put a safe distance between my sanity and my old anchor.

TIME fucked me over and now, it was my turn to be on top! To maintain the new speed was not something I could be sure of, but I had no other choice. She was either kind enough to let me win this one or so surprised that she will just let it go. I survived and got out of it stronger. I know that she will be getting her revenge, I am still looking forward to see where it will come from.

You see, the *dance of seduction* with *TIME* is a never-ending one and will always keep evolving. Pleasure and distress, desire, and pain are in the mix. The only time where my victory was clear and definitive was a win given by the *Angel of Life* as she gave me a son. Until I hold him in my arms, *TIME* was laughing at me. But then, as he opened his eyes to look at me for the first time, *TIME* suddenly became a shadow in the back of the room.

The day my son was born, that day changed everything. Suddenly I became aware of my expiration date and at the same time, to be able to provide and to love him, I found more and more ways to create more time in a day. It is when

I started to gain *momentum* and to cheat on *TIME*. Not simply like before, but now with more and more ease.

Holding that little head sleeping in the palm of my hand, I changed perspective, I changed life. If only he will be doing back to me half of what I did to my parents, I will be the luckiest of parents… His birth brought me closer to the gratitude I owe to my own parents.

Holding him close to my chest, I also realized that I could be the hardest of father and that could drive an edge between us. If I march the same path as my parents, I will pass on to him much of my expectations and dreams in life, only to see good intentions turned into poisons. I've been there, and I am made pretty strong.

Instead of putting on him the burden of expectations, that morning looking at the sunrise from my condo-hotel lounge, I made a decision while kissing his forehead. I will be fathering by example, preaching the values by my actions, not my words.

My parents taught me to be strong and smart. That strength was eventually the biggest edge between my father and myself. I will do better, I will teach my son *generosity* and *flexibility* instead.

Generosity, I knew. But *flexibility*… that was something I had to learn. Today I am a better, bigger man thanks to that morning. William, my son, is now 8 and the plan is working!

He has grown smart and strong as baselines, but furthermore, *generosity* is a personality trait and *flexibility*, he is about to master. To him, it is called having an open mind. Since he was 5, he had to learn the concept.

The best proof I can give you is this. A night when he was 7, out of nowhere, he said from the backseat of the car as we were driving home: "Papa, when I'll be big, I wanted to write two books. One about being a good son and one about a lion heart!" I was writing my third book by then, talking about leadership and lion hearts. My wife and I shared tears of joy.

I picked on the cues and started talking and exchanging with him. To make sure that I wasn't pulling on him, I reserved the positions and put him in the driver's seat.

The next morning, I woke him up saying that he will not be writing about a lion heart since that was my book. Instead, he can write about a chicken heart! That got him red of anger and he argued and argued about why it should be him writing the lion heart's book. To make peace, we arrived with this story together:

Everybody is born little, like a chicken. As some will open up their heart, they will grow into a lion heart. If they aren't open, they will stay small and remain a chicken. He loved it! A year later, his book is still to be written. He's 8, he has all the time to write his masterpiece without being late.

That's how kind *TIME* was to me as I became a dad. Actually, I have noticed a weak spot in her heart. Every time I wasn't at the centre of the attention or the effort, she was kinder and more generous. That's how we shared some love in our desired and opulent relationship.

Each time, it was about me, solely me, she became that same bitch trying to put a leash and a knife on my throat. Instead of blaming her for her cruelty and double personality, I learnt to leverage over her weak spot.

"I FOUND MY WORTH IN THE SERVICE OF OTHERS."
Dr. BAK NGUYEN

To cheat *TIME* and to leave forever, this is my take. So far it worked like a charm. I am not sure that I will ever beat *TIME* completely nor that I want to do that. I have grown dependent on the spices and waves of this extra-conjugal relationship.

To have a lover as *TIME* is what keeps me on my toes and what's giving me my extra edge. I don't know exactly what I bring to her from the relationship, but to sleep with a *force of nature* is surely not a small thing.

Even figuratively, it makes sense and explains a lot. The wording is not just for the lyricism and the style, they are the reality: I have the ability to draft and redraft.

Everything has a price and I will still have to face the *Angel of Life*, the kind and loving angel who bed with me first... But *TIME* as a mistress and a lover who was well worth the risk and the anger.

To be continued.

This is **FORCES OF NATURE**. Welcome to the Alphas.

> ALL MY CHALLENGES
> WERE THE BIGGEST
> AS I FACED THEM
> AND VAGUE SOUVENIRS
> AS I MOVED ON
>
> Dr. BAK NGUYEN

CHAPTER 4 - TRUTH

"TO FACE TRUTH IS A NECESSARY EVIL TO KEEP ONE HUMBLE AND PREPARE ONE TO EVENTUALLY FACE GOD."

DR. BAK NGUYEN

The more I advanced on my journey, the more subtle and vicious can be the *Forces of Nature* opposing me. *Inertia* was an intimidating mountain, but once I left it behind, it stays behind. *Myopia* is like cancer, we never know when it will come back striking. The only remedy is to stay aware and humble.

Until now, it was hard enough, but the fight was fair, the forces of opposition were at least identifiable and from the outside. Then, comes the *Angel of TIME*, that lover who either corrupted us or inspire us or both, all at once.

Even the wording is perplexing since we do not know how to react to her. And she keeps changing moods and desires. In the mythology, this is where the concept of *Demon* starts to elude the concept of *Angel*.

> "DEMON AND ANGEL ARE TWO AND ONE AT THE SAME TIME."
> Dr. BAK NGUYEN

Is it *Myopia* that is the cause of our duo vision? It must be them who are playing with us, those *Forces of Nature* laughing at us. All my mentors will slap me in the back of the head telling me to man up and to take responsibility.

If the *Forces of Nature* had two faces, it was for me to understand and analyze carefully the situation before engaging with them. They are absolutely right! The only blames that are useful is the ones I assigned to myself. Not for the pleasure of self-inflicting wounds but to realize where I went wrong and how I got improved on my behaviours and reflexes. That's the only way to genuinely leverage on each of our steps, wins, and failures.

> **" KNOW WHO YOU ARE, KNOW WHO YOU ARE DEALING WITH, AND THEN, DEAL!"**
> Dr. BAK NGUYEN

Sure That brings us to the next *Forces of Nature* to face and to triumph from *Truth*, a cold unforgiven spectre. To stand in front of *Truth*, one feels both naked and small, infinitely small. That was just as we faced with the spectre of *Truth*. But it gets even more intimidating as we need to show up in its trial court.

Set in stone and so cold that life itself never joins in, *Truth* is not a friendly face. Actually, the *Angel of Truth* has no face and many faces, all at once. When stared in the face of *Truth*, what we really see is the reflection of what we are, without filters, without charismatic lighting, without forgiving shadows. The cold hard truth!

There are so many faces to the truth and there is always that void behind the projection or the void between what we are and what we were destined for. *Truth* is a void, that is why it feels so cold!

The *void of Truth* will swallow us alive if we stare into its eyes for too long. That's a certainty. But over time, the stronger we get, the longer we might stand its look before getting swallowed. Swallowed, not even eaten since *Truth* won't give us that much attention.

I really don't know how *Truth* has such good press within our societies as an *Angel of Light*? It surely is a source of Light, the cold neon kind, showing all imperfections on corpses in the coroner's office. You get the image.

> "NOT ALL TRUTHS ARE USEFUL. ONE MUST STAND READY FIRST."
> Dr. BAK NGUYEN

We are not talking about lying here, it was just us and the *Angel of Truth*. It is about what can be useful to keep us in evolution and to push us forward on the path of our destiny.

What I've learnt is to pick a staring contest with *Truth* is as stupid as to have that same contest with Medusa, the greek monster that turns every living soul into stone as they look at her. Both *Truth* and Medusa are ugly and, without a single word, they will entrap us in a body of stone for Medusa and a heart of stone in the case of *Truth*. I really do not know if those two are related somehow...

> "STARING IN THE EYES OF TRUTH FOR TOO LONG WILL CHANGE YOUR HEART INTO A HEART OF STONE."
> Dr. BAK NGUYEN

From that, a new challenge emerges: the challenge to remain in control and unchanged by the event. The strength and determination to keep what I deem good and kind in my heart to simply ignore those who are trying to break or knock me down.

> "YOU WILL NOT ERASE THAT SMILE ON MY FACE NOR THE LIGHT OF JOY AND HOPE IN MY HEART."
> Dr. BAK NGUYEN

I came in contact with *Truth* from within my first moments alive. That warm and reassuring love from my mother was a great comfort, only to be violently separated from it later on. Then, from the same person I was looking up for comfort and pure love came the expectations and the breaking down of my wings.

She gave me her love but also transferred down her fears and doubts. My father protected me from those, only to replace them with even bigger ones…

To be fair, as awared and carefully that I can be, I am doing more or less the same to my son. That seems like a fatality and a flaw within our belief system.

I first thought it was the work of *Inertia* throwing doubt, fear, and ignorance at us. But even when I finally move on and left the mountain of *Inertia* behind, the *cold shadow of reflection* was still there. Very present.

> "TRUTH IS THE COLD AND DIVINE REFLECTION OF WHAT AND WHO WE ARE."
> Dr. BAK NGUYEN

That's why it is so hard to fight with *Truth* since we are fighting ourselves. We are doing so within the worst conditions ever: fighting our biggest void as we are left small and naked, often humiliated.

In my previous book, I mention the *shield of Pride* which we all misuse in our everyday lives as we use it to face each other. That shield is the only weapon that will give us a chance facing with *Truth*, and *Truth* alone.

> "THE SHIELD OF PRIDE IS THE ONLY WEAPON
> OF USE IN FRONT OF TRUTH, THE ANGEL."
> Dr. BAK NGUYEN

And again, to hold that shield too tight and for too long will have as much damages as to stare in the *eyes of Truth* itself! The shield will buy us some time to get out of the face-off and to regroup.

A very different reality than those related in Greek Mythology: we do not have to cut off the head of the monster Medusa to triumph, we simply need to survive our encounter, stronger and a little wiser. We have to be careful not to piss off the *Angel* either since we will be back in its courtroom sooner than we might want.

> "ONE CANNOT KILL A FORCE OF NATURE.
> ONE SIMPLY MUST GROW INTO ONE TO STOP THE THREATS."
> Dr. BAK NGUYEN

In a beautiful portrait, that is my relationship with the *Angel of Truth*, the *Force of Nature* which I cannot ever win over neither leave behind. If anything, its role is to remind me of my own littleness and by how far I have advanced since our last encounter in its courtroom.

If in my life, I am always focusing on what I haven't yet accomplished, in its presence, I find comfort looking at what I've accomplished. That's my *shield of Pride*. With time, my shield is getting bigger and shinier.

Within my last encounters with *Truth*, I even avoid crossing its look since I was too tired and handicapped by my own trials and open quests. I simply have a peak of its presence through the reflection from my shield. But looking for too long at my shield, it loses its shine, and rust starts to appear. Is that the effect of *Truth* or of my own corruption?

Trust me, in that courtroom, you do not have enough time to sit on that kind of philosophical question. Even if I write books and I am sharing my thoughts with you, I am, at my core, a very practical person: everything I do has a purpose and a reason.

> "IF I DON'T KNOW IT YET, I'LL FIND OUT LATER. I DID IT BECAUSE I FELT IT."
> Dr. BAK NGUYEN

That's my truth and I have finally come around to accept it. To understand that I will never find rest until I face the ultimate trial before God, asking me to show what I've done with what I've received. Until that day, I will stand unsatisfied.

Actually, I will stand with fear, since that is the only deep fear I have from this life: to face God and to be lesser than his expectations. I've been told that God is good and kind. Until I am standing in his presence, I rehearse my trial with my forced companion, the *Angel of Truth*.

And I get better and better, facing its judgment and reflections. Even if its presence takes a huge token on my energy, I made my peace with that necessary evil. I welcome our Teatime together.

That's how I have come around to see my audiences within the *courtroom of Truth*. I boil the water, infuse the Tea. As the infusion is perfect, I enjoy my cup of tea, carefully keeping my eye on my cup and politely excuse myself by the end of my cup. I do so with calm and without rushing.

Like any Angels, *Truth* can sense Fear and will feed on it. Throughout the years, I came in with my *shield of Pride*. Since I am bringing my *teapot*, I even leave the shield at the door lately. I am not sure that it is wise or even safe, but I needed to evolve and lazy as I am, caring that shield around was becoming a bigger and bigger burden. Especially the time I need to spend to polish it and to clean it after each encounter in the courtroom...

Now, with a cup of tea, I practically have nothing to do after leaving the courtroom. On that, I now better enjoy my encounters with the Angel of Truth. But to use the word

ENJOY is not very respectful since it is closer to a big fat lie! I have accepted the *Truth*, not enjoyed it!

> "TO FACE TRUTH IS A NECESSARY EVIL TO KEEP ONE HUMBLE AND PREPARE ONE TO EVENTUALLY FACE GOD."
> Dr. BAK NGUYEN

For that, I am grateful. That is how I keep on track my ledger, the achievements, the collaterals, and how heavy is still the void, my void on the balance. There is no balance of justice, at least not that I have seen. There is just the *balance of Truth*: on one side the void of our unachieved destiny and on the other, our ledger.

To be realistic, I never really saw a significant movement from as far as I can remember. I told you, *Truth* is a cold heart son of a bitch! And we do not even have the luxury to say that it was a lie and that it was playing us…

> "TRUTH MAY NOT BE PRETTY BUT IT IS NO DEVIL."
> Dr. BAK NGUYEN

That's my truth. To know that this will only end the day I face God, the day Life will leave me. My task is a never-ending one. My destiny is to never find rest nor satisfaction.

My curse is that I am blessed with multiple talents and skills and from each, I must find use and dividends.

The more I put them at use, the more wins I accumulate. Sometimes, from those wins, I discover new skills. For a minute or two, I am as excited as a kid opening up a new toy! A newfound power! But every single time, *Truth* comes hurrying back at the door reminding me that I must now find new dividends to honour those shiny new skills!

I am borrowing from God, and I can cease the contract nor change the terms, he alone has that power. For now, I have a great credit score on his books and he still favours me with more credits. That's the cold hard truth.

Towards God, I am both fearful and grateful. To the *Angel of Truth*, I hate its guts but I am glad that I have something to blame and hate, keeping God out of my emotions.

To the *Angel of Time*, I need her attention to replenish both my ambitions and sense of urgency. She is my leverage upon myself in the whole system. I know I will die one day, but until it is over, it is my job to keep delivering.

Make it happen!

This is **FORCES OF NATURE**. Welcome to the Alphas.

ALL MY CHALLENGES WERE THE BIGGEST AS I FACED THEM AND VAGUE SOUVENIRS AS I MOVED ON

Dr. BAK NGUYEN

TWO FACES

CHAPTER 5 - TWO FACES
"NO ONE CAN BE POWERFUL BY HIMSELF. IMAGINE HALF OF HIM...
WHAT CHANCE DOES HE HAS?"
DR. BAK NGUYEN

There are at least two sides to everyone and to everything. To start with this in mind, we have already handicapped ourselves to believe and to build faith in Life and in ourselves.

> " IN ORDER FOR ONE TO BELIEVE,
> THERE MUST BE NO DOUBT, THEREFORE, NO BUT. "
> Dr. BAK NGUYEN

Two Faces is messing with our heads and the founding of our convictions. That is why all geniuses started as crazy people until they completely gave up on the authorities and on *Conformity*. Only then, will some prevail and come back to save us. The amazement in all of it was that they are still taking the time to come back to save the rest of us.

Those who didn't prevail, just went their way, leaving us to our pain and with our doubts. Can we blame them? With everything that we made them endure! Thanks to those who came back, we may have a fighting chance to survive as a species and a chance for happiness as individuals. We must honour their generosity by following in their footsteps: to grow bigger and more generous than the welcomes reserved to us.

A few years ago, I started my training to join the political class. My mentor and coach told me that it takes a crazy person with a sense of naivety to survive in the political realm since everyone will have you back and then, eat on it. That's part of the game.

The last thing we need is to be affected by it. But we can also not take it for a fact, and jump in joyfully, thinking that we can change the world for the better! To join to change the world, if not this, what else are we joining for?

The greatest of his teaching was to take me on my specific words: to change the world, which world are you referring to? And as we philosophized, I realized that I had the magical **capacity to heal** and to **edit my story**. The scars are still there, but the pain and the souvenirs are faded aways in the back-scene.

Even if my enhanced sense of Empathy makes me feel everyone's desires and pains, I also have the ability to make complete abstraction of the facts and to move unburden, or almost. I have not been always like this, but through much pain and deception, I've learnt, learnt to accept myself for who I was, and learnt to not expect more from others.

> "EVEN IF THEY DON'T LIKE ME,
> THAT DOESN'T MEAN THAT I'LL STOP CARING."
> Dr. BAK NGUYEN

A few years ago, I literally worked to save a life. People were begging for my involvement even if I did not see how I could be of use.. I went all in and drove the ball out of sight, further than even the general public can understand. So far that I attracted the attention of some of the masters in the game. One of them is today a mentor and close friend.

Except for that friendship, most people concerned eventually played against me, once they did need me no more. I saved a life and my work held the promise to save many more for the years to come… I was simply naive to think that if you are doing good and serve others, they will come to embrace you. How wrong I was. There are two faces to each coin, to each soul.

Life is a delicate balance and a series of choices. I unbalanced myself to evolve, this time on demand, but I unbalanced what was delicate and I did not fully understand all its implications, not on the grand scheme of things nor on the logic, but on the individual levels, of how each person would be feeling about the matter and the solution. *Jealousy* and *lust of power* may be ugly but they are very punctual to show up. They rarely miss out on an occasion, any occasion.

For as long as the pain is not greater than the *pain of change*, people will be fighting to stand still, even in the mud. That was their first face. Then, the second one showed up.

Not everyone is equal in this life. We were born with unique skills and potentials, everyone can matter and fight for their worth, but not everyone has the same potential nor does that matter. That's potential, imagine all of those too afraid to live up to their destiny... those are even nastier.

Before, I took it personally and took it upon my shoulders to save everyone, at least those I can identify. Weren't we all raised like that, to lend a hand when asked for? But eventually, I came to my senses.

I will always be there to help because I can. Simply because I can and it is in my nature to do so. But I also have to preserve my destiny, to help the many. So now, I lend my hand, but not to the extent to endanger my position nor to change the course of my *momentum*.

Realizing how much I have changed cost me a few nights of sleep. And then, my actions started to change the world, for the better... I try every day to remind myself of my mission and of who I am to not get lost in the *Mirage* from my own *Shield of Pride*.

I hold *Gratitude* and *Loyalty* as the most precious values I've received from my time in *Conformity* to remind me that I was once, one of them. That is how I became truly humble. And because there were a few people who are also different, who lent a hand, sometimes complete strangers, who went on to save the day... I have to honour them.

I know now, I am one of those people. My mission is to rise up and then, raise the average with me. Not all at once, but in due and given time: when the pain will be great enough to require a doctor. And a doctor, they made out of me.

Is *TWO FACES* a Force of Nature like other angels and demons? *TWO FACES* is like the *Angel of Truth*, it is a part of us. The process in which, in order to understand things and to accommodate it to our simple minds, we needed to cut everything into smaller pieces, in two. The light and the darkness, the good and the bad, the material and the energy... it was, and still, is at its original one.

So *TWO FACES* is a creature of our own limitations and destiny, to be human. It now stands as tall and as powerful as any of the other *Forces of Nature*. What does that tell us? That we are not as weak nor as small as we believe since our own creation and beliefs gave birth to a *Force of Nature*.

We are made weak since that same *Force of Nature* is cutting us in half as we grew in size and in strength. To cut the darkness out, to carve the animal instinct out, to chase the impurities of our thoughts... instead of mastering our attributes and nature, we cut out half of ourselves to differentiate and we then developed the bad habit to leverage from the differentiation to evolve. We did this since the age of the hunter and the caveman. It is now in our DNA.

The main flaw of that practice is that what we cut off was a part of ourselves and is still linked somehow to us, even if we discarded them at the bottom of the ocean. Like invisible anchors, they will have their ways to hold us down and to eventually pull us from our rise to the clouds. Not by revenge, but by nature. We were, and are, one. Even if we do not see it clearly.

> " NO ONE CAN BE POWERFUL BY HIMSELF. IMAGINE HALF OF HIM...
> WHAT CHANCE DOES HE HAS? "
> Dr. BAK NGUYEN

To be whole is to accept who we are. We must stop feeding *TWO FACES*, its dichotomy, and obsession to *Bonzai* each of our limbs. The first clue of wholeness is the chance to happiness, a real and genuine chance. Once whole, so then what? Being dismembered and forced into survival mode, we, as a species, have developed a strength that allowed us to give birth to a *Force of Nature*!

That strength is called *cooperation*, the *power of connections*. As we network, we found ways to connect and to share our vital energy to evolve. Together, we go further... but that network is also called *Conformity*!

If at first, our diminished soul felt the need for connections, eventually, it must find the courage and the strength to heal and to patch itself up to be whole again. And then, it can either just go free or it can be the bigger and greater one and come back to raise the average and to support the mean.

Not just to prove wrong all of those who are messing with its head or spitting on its name, but to give a chance to others likeminded, a hope and a way to contribute back.

> "AFTER THE HEALING, ONCE WHOLE, ALL THERE ARE, ARE CHOICES."
> Dr. BAK NGUYEN

Even Life has two faces... The *Angel* we married and loved, that *Angel* is just half of what she really is. She never hides her half away, we were too simple-minded to grasp her entirely. She loves and nurtures. She also let us be. And we came up with false beliefs to ease our minds and to facilitate our belief system.

The *Angel of Death* was Fear taking on a bigger role than itself, to gain importance. And *Fear* started with *Doubts* at its core. A simple tread of insecurity that we breathed to life as we kept it alive. Part of Doubt became strong enough to find root in our heart. That's when the seed was planted. Fear became real, a new species born from the power of the mind, Doubt, and the flesh of passion, our heart.

Today, both **Fear** and **Doubt** have the power of the *Forces of Nature*, because we gave it to them and forgot how it all started. We are such simple minds that we even let **FEAR** to corrupt and take over a place in our bed!

Yes, the *Angel of Life* that we love and married is actually also the *Angel of Death*! A kind and soft Angel seeing the magic of creation following its course. But for most of our life, we were sleeping with **FEAR** in disguise. Can you see the power we each hold? And how we have forgotten who and what we are?

We have the power to make a *Force of Nature*. We might be one for all that we know. But to find out who and what we are, we must remember and wake up. We must stop the dichotomizations and the differentiation.

I do not fight *TWO FACES*, that will be a waste of my time and intelligence. I will be looking for my whole, for my time to heal and once I will have patch myself up to be whole and happy, I will go back to help my kind to find their way.

This is my blessing and I fully accept it, now that I understand.

This is **FORCES OF NATURE**. Welcome to the Alphas.

ALL MY CHALLENGES WERE THE BIGGEST AS I FACED THEM AND VAGUE SOUVENIRS AS I MOVED ON

Dr. BAK NGUYEN

CHAPTER 6 - EMOTIONS
"DOMESTICATION IS AN UNNATURAL AND CRUEL PROCESS"
DR. BAK NGUYEN

> **" THERE IS NO BIGGER FOE THAN THE ONE WITHIN."**
> Dr. BAK NGUYEN

Emotions are what make us unique and real. Love, happiness, jealousy, envy are each, powerful motivators of human behaviours. If we hold any strength from nature, *Emotions* are it! What is giving us our edge and our unpredictability are the emotions we embody. In a word, our humanity.

Know how to empower your *Emotions,* and to channel their energy and you will be propelled into your destiny. Just like in every quest, we are facing the *Titans* and the *Monsters*, but we've also received the gift of powerful allies. *Emotions* are the beast inside, the brute force that will come out to save the day... if we stay in control.

That beast coming out, we can all choose its form and shape. If there is something most of us know is that we have the choice of what will be coming out. Is it going to be a stallion, a tiger, or a bear, it is for us to decide. The problem occur when we were concentrating all of our attention to hold it still and try to contain the steam in, from our training for *Conformity*.

Emotions are two faces creatures. First, they defined us and gave us our motivation and individuality. And then, they pushed us forward to walk our talk and thoughts. Their nature is to amplify and exaggerate everything, often making what was first right and justified, overdosed, and inappropriate.

And they are doing nothing, it is us that are to blame. We went too far! It was either this or we risked doing nothing, standing still facing the events. *Emotions* are hormones, and to all of those studying medicine, hormonal responses are **all or nothing**. So is the answer related to the stimulus, all or nothing?

> "POWER IS ABOUT USEFULNESS, NOT DEMONSTRATION."
> Dr. BAK NGUYEN

The more the hormones, the greater the beast? Not necessarily. The better the channelling, the more powerful the beast. To tame that beast, one has to train himself to live with his emotions. To not hold them back or to ignore them since he will be turning them from an ally into a foe. Ever heard the saying *"to go with the flow"* or *"to follow the wind"*? To stand against our own, is simply contra-productive and plain stupid.

Mount the beast, but be in control. You control the beast yourself, that's the only way. Be weak and you'll be the beast, a real beast that people will call monster and you will be hunted down. You see, the beast was your body reacting, for as long as your head and your heart are in control, you are telling the beast what to do.

Emotions were the boost to get the « *Hulk* » out. The motivation should be well-identified within our heart and the mapping of its execution, well planned within our head. As everything is in order, the beast of *Emotions*, once out, is what will make the *Forces of Nature* bow down.

Emotions are in, they are part of us, they are forcing us to see bigger than our daily dimension. To use them facing the *Forces of Nature*, one can do no wrong but to practice to tame and to master the beast inside, to channel the energy, and to harness its usefulness.

To unleash against another human being or even worst, to burst in the face of loved ones, are the kind of atrocities that will plan the *seeds of regrets* and *fear* deep into one soul and handicap it seriously.

We all did it. We all leashed out on our loved ones. We all did tremendous damages to those we cherish the most. They weren't the enemies, we were. Out of guilt and shame, *Conformity* gave us a knife to cut down our wings, our fences, our limbs. And we did.

> **" DOMESTICATION IS AN UNNATURAL AND CRUEL PROCESS."**
> Dr. BAK NGUYEN

And yet, we are domesticating ourselves to try to fit inside of an enclosed area. Why are we so cheap? All we needed was some space and the time to run the course of our *Emotions* until the hormones run out. It is healthy both spiritually and physically. But we somehow falsely thought that we can **entrap the beast within obesity**, throwing guilt and procrastination to bury it. Are we that naive?

> **"IT'S CRAZY HOW WE CAN BE OUR GREATEST ENEMY."**
> Dr. BAK NGUYEN

Learn to know yourself first! To know and to control the beast inside is amongst the first steps. Go out there and play with the big ones, the *Forces of Nature*, instead of practicing on the other unsecured beings surrounding you, each more perplexed than the other, unchecked on their own powers.

To go out and to face Nature is the only sain way to unleash the full might of our emotions, and to have the time and opportunity to observe them, to tame and master them.

We need space and time. That is called *Freedom*. We need to grow powerful enough to mount the beast. This is called *Confidence*. We need to channel the energy to find its worth. This is called *Power*.

We are creatures of Nature and inside of each of us, we are holding its wonders. Forget about tuning it down and ignoring our own greatness. Be confident and kind enough to let it be, in a safe environment, in Nature, not inside the enclosure of domestication.

Sure, it will take time and much energy to tame that beast inside. Eventually, you will need to feed that beast and grow with it. My beast is a *Tornado* called *momentum*. It started as a burst of energy-burning all around, people and things. Then, I learnt to put the heat behind to avoid being burn. From it, I found an amazing force of propulsion. But I was destroying my room and home as I practiced inside.

To solve both the bursting and its collaterals, I went out, to test my strengths and to get to know my beast. That's when I started to leverage my emotions to get things done.

When the task given didn't need much power, I channelled the emotions to produce speed. Since the results can not be more than a predefined one, at least, that way I can beat the expectations by finishing it faster. That is how I came up with my **definition of laziness**: to get out of a task a fast as possible.

"TO DEVELOP MY INNER POWERS, I EMBRACED LAZINESS."
Dr. BAK NGUYEN

So I trained inside a classrooms, inside of books, and inside of my mind. The classrooms and the books were sometimes torn apart as I couldn't hold and channel all of the beasts. My mind grew faster and bigger than expected.

The greater the beast, the larger was my mind. Usually, the fish will grow as much as the bowl. This time, the bowl was growing to accommodate the fast-growing beast. And the bowl was my mind! It became the safe ground on which I could let go freely and not have any regrets.

I still need to know what to do with all the newly found powers…

You see, we are a whole living in harmony, that's the magic of Life. If we stop the practice of *"Bonzaing"* our soul and body, we are one flowing free within the Universe, with the Universe. The moment we are whole and acting as one, we are vibrating at our unique frequency. That frequency is happiness and will join in with the Universe, in synergy.

That's how I escaped. That's how I saved my wings from total amputation. That's how I healed from the regrets, ignoring the guilt and mounting my inner beast. To compensate for my incapacitated half amputated wings, I compensated by running fast.

Fast enough to be able to fly, differently, from the power of *Momentum*! I grew from *burst* to *speed* and from *speed* to *momentum*. Today, I can deploy a *Tornado* inside of a boardroom and get people energized and inspired. In truth, they are feeling the vibration of my bass, the treble of my vision, and they feel empowered by the possibilities of their own power!

> "EMOTIONS ARE HORMONAL RESPONSES. THE RECIPE AND THE DOSAGE ARE OUR IDENTITIES."
> Dr. BAK NGUYEN

In other words, the beast is our Identity. Cut it off, and you have an empty name, maybe even a useless name. How do we dose an *all or nothing equation?* By balancing it with equals, with more and more equations.

Train in safe spaces, inside of abundance and freedom. Those, you might find in your mind or in your heart. If not, borrow someone else's mind. Don't be afraid, the fun is growing as you share both your feelings and the excitement.

Let go first and then observe. Soon enough, you will be mounting your beast, your power. Embrace your power by letting them be. Love yourself by respecting your true nature, what you've received from birth, your Emotions. And please, do not feed on regrets, do not test and unleash your powers on your loved ones. Only guilt and amputation will come out of the sad experience.

Will Emotions be an ally or a foe to oppose, it is a choice no one can make but you. Know that it is possible to be one with the beast and still be kind and gentle.

Actually, the beast has more usefulness than the *"Bonzaied"* civilized peer feeding with envy and jealousy, trying to drown his own pain away. The pain wasn't there at the origin. We made it permanent as we refused the *Force of Nature* within and then, took actions against it, against ourselves.

Learn to know and to respect yourself.

This is **FORCES OF NATURE**. Welcome to the Alphas.

> ALL MY CHALLENGES
> WERE THE BIGGEST
> AS I FACED THEM
> AND VAGUE SOUVENIRS
> AS I MOVED ON
>
> Dr. BAK NGUYEN

CHAPTER 7 - EXPECTATIONS

"LOVE COMES IN ALL SAUCES, SOMETIMES, IT WAS ALSO WRAPPED WITH BITTERNESS AND NOSTALGIA. SO EXPECTATION TOOK SEEDS."

DR. BAK NGUYEN

We had a break in the last chapter, having found a *Force of Nature* to ally ourselves with, our *inner beast*. Please don't get used to the gifts, there are rare and often wrapped within much, much work, energy, and efforts.

The next *Force of Nature* we will be opposing is even a harder one to fight since we do not see it. But trust me, it is pretty real and powerful! It was born from our parents and transferred to us with natural means, wrapped with love and tenderness.

> "LOVE COMES IN ALL SAUCES, SOMETIMES, WRAPPED WITH BITTERNESS AND NOSTALGIA."
> Dr. BAK NGUYEN

Not all parents have the same tastes and habits... but like a virus, it was willingly given to us, injected into us to fight *Inertia*. They planted the seeds deep in our hearts, the *seeds of Expectation*. On one side, they were wishing nothing but the best for us. On the other, they were asking us to stand in line and to forget about our inner Forces and Nature. And so the conflict began, in the name of Love.

> "TO PLEASE THEM OR TO LISTEN TO OURSELVES, THAT IS THE QUESTION?"
> Dr. BAK NGUYEN

Each of us marched uphill to face that battle. To please in the name of Love is the *virus of Expectation*. To change and to amputate in the name of Love are the symptoms of the *infection of Expectation*. To scar for life is the *mark of Expectation*.

> "FEW WILL HEAL COMPLETELY FROM THE INFECTION OF EXPECTATION. FOR THE REST OF THEIR LIVES, THEY MIGHT BE CHASING GHOSTS."
> Dr. BAK NGUYEN

A few of us are lucky enough to have parents who knew better, parents who took the time and effort to identify our strengths and nature. They wished for us the best, not what they couldn't achieve in their lives but what we hold the potential to.

Honour them, be grateful and thankful. We were not the norm but the exceptions, the few exceptions. If that has been your case, know that your parents took a stand against *Conformity* to give you a starting chance to happiness, to find yourself and to define.

> "THE RESULT WAS CONFIDENCE, STRONG AND PURE SELF, CONFIDENCE."
> Dr. BAK NGUYEN

They still transferred *Expectations*, but the virus was not as virulent not hold the same damaging potential to afflict our *Confidence*. Often, all it did was to give us a choice, an opportunity to make up our mind, from freedom, with confidence. *Confidence* is the **gateway to our identity**, break it and the doors will close down forever.

For a mind forever undersieged, *Death* and *Starvation* will occur, maybe later than expected, but it will occur. To a heart under siege, each beating becomes a bearing of burdens, of the weight of the Universe. That is what they saved us from, unrealistic and generic Expectations.

> "TO FLY, ONE MUST BE LIGHT. TO SPEED, ONE MUST CUT THE DEAD WEIGHTS. THOSE LUCKIEST HAD NOTHING TO CUT!"
> Dr. BAK NGUYEN

To the average parents, the average children, and the common virus. Expectations can come from many sources. If our parents were not strong enough to take a stand, they are letting the flow taking over their daily life, they will be transferring the trending virus. *Conformity* is very powerful using that means to connect and to average most of its people, *Expectations* and then, *Fear*.

Actually, *Conformity* started first with *Expectations*, injecting it with large doses as we were standing in line from our youth.

Often, our parents were begging for it since *Expectations* were falsely called *Hope* and wrapped with much Love. Like any virus, our body will start producing antibodies to fight the intrusion.

Those antibodies were ways for our body to grow and to adapt. Since we were fighting them, they found ways to suppress our natural reaction with obstruction and amputations. Their mean was another virus called *Guilt*! And we lined up for that injection too! We had no choice, in the name of *Love* and of *God*.

Ever read a medieval story about how medicine was practiced back then? To fight a fever, we were taking litres of blood from the body to diminish the pressure... Basically, we were weakening a body already under attack. To save it, we were killing it.

Even today, still a big part of medicine is the science to cut off something from the whole. Strange comparison, but in the same period, as the plague was menacing humankind, the religions killed more souls than the terrifying illness.

False expectations had planted a very bad habit into our culture as a collectivity: every time something is weak, we start cutting it into smaller pieces... to help it, to kill it. With this key, start looking around you and you'll realize that we may have made much progress in medicine and in science, but the virus is still part of our DNA and the culture hasn't changed much since.

> "IT WAS DONE IN GOOD FAITH, BUT WITH SUCH IGNORANCE THEN. SO IT IS WITH THE VIRUS OF EXPECTATION TODAY, IN GOOD FAITH BUT WITH SUCH IGNORANCE STILL."
> Dr. BAK NGUYEN

Ever saw someone dying from the inside? The sweat is burning the skin as it comes slightly in contact with. The burns are so subtle that he is convinced that he is not sick! Just getting through a bad day. That day then becomes months and years, eating him up from inside. Yes, he feels that something is wrong but what? He was always like this for as long as he can remember...

Eventually, he will fight back, but he will soon realize the siege he was defending was a lie, a big fat lie. The enemy from the other side never intended to get in, up until that point. The only result was to interrupt the arrival of food and provisions from the outside to prevent any growth. Then, slowly the starvation started.

> "TO KILL A MIND, GET IT TO THINK IN POOR WAYS: TO DIVIDE AND SUBTRACT."
> Dr. BAK NGUYEN

Remember that we all have beasts inside of us? What happens when beasts are unleashed within a close, too close area? They destroy and disturb everyone and everything.

Imagine with scarce and precious resources laying around... So we turn the knife on them.

Fear and *Paranoia* will take care of the rest... of the self-destruction. This can kill a city. The same strategy will kill a spirit and a body, silently, slowly, and efficiently. Viruses.

Expectations are nothing more than viruses. Expectations coming from oneself is *Ambition*. But Ambitions passing down from one generation to the next are simply Expectations. And Expectations are viruses.

> "MAKE LEVERAGE OUT OF EACH OF YOUR LIABILITIES TO MOVE FORWARD."
> Dr. BAK NGUYEN

So how do we fight that illness eating us from inside? I made my choice to become a dentist to please the dream of my parents. Expectations, check! Then, I didn't follow through with my opportunity to go to Hollywood to become a movie producer, again to ease my parents and my girlfriend, whom I eventually married.

To be honest, I was exhausted after the release of my first film and I badly needed moral support. The support wasn't there, I chickened out facing the unknown, my destiny. From that regret, I nearly threw my entire life away.

I came back to Canada to be a dentist. I had much to lose not to succeed. So I built **Mdex**, my dental company, serving people. But my heart wasn't there. This time, I was facing the burden of my own *Expectations* and *deceptions*.

For the first time in my life, my ambitions weren't propelling me, but instead, they were holding my head underwater. The *Expectations* to live the dream of my parents first and then, the inability to live up to my own. I paid the price of *Expectations,* twice!

I ended up signing a contract with myself for 10 years, putting aside, at least, the *burden of expectations* coming from my failed dreams. I rolled up my sleeves and put my patients at the centre of my attention. I became a successful and appreciated dentist. I am not the best, I am the kind doctor who delivers! That's who they trusted.

I spent more than 20 years in the profession, from dental school to CEO. I learnt the profession inside and out and today, I took all of my experiences healing from the *burden of Expectations* to develop new ways to practice and to deliver dentistry. I hated what I was doing, but I did it so my time was worthwhile, delivering results and happiness.

Today, my company has the chance to rewrite the history of my industries, and by doing so, I will have changed the world for the better. How did I do it? By **leveraging my pain** to find a solution to remedy it. I leveraged off of the scars and wounds of *Expectation* to understand my pain and the pain of others.

Today, I've healed and I know a way to heal. That's what I am sharing with the world, the Hope that there is a way out. *The virus of Expectations* is today my main ally since it went rogue and afflicted everyone. Since the illness is universal, all I had to do was to identify it clearly and let my training as a doctor to take over.

To diagnose, treat and reevaluate. Everywhere science reached a limit, I had my creativity to help me link the dots and to find new ways to cope. From the worst burden on my back, twice, today the virus of Expectations is serving my message of Hope.

This is ironic since I will be serving *Expectations* its own medicine, to penetrate and get defeat from the inside out. *Hope* is the message that the virus is delivering now. The bigger the pain, the greater the need for hope. And *Hope*, I embody, not just from my words but from my work and sharing.

When I said that the *Forces of Nature* are playing with me, today, they have to deal with me and everything I learnt, playing with them. I am the *Hope* that Humanity is more than just Apes fighting to reproduce and differentiate amongst themselves. From *Expectations*, I grew stronger. I guess I must be grateful... to have survived such training.

Hope is coming.

This is **FORCES OF NATURE**. Welcome to the Alphas.

ALL MY CHALLENGES
WERE THE BIGGEST
AS I FACED THEM
AND VAGUE SOUVENIRS
AS I MOVED ON

Dr. BAK NGUYEN

CHAPTER 8 - ABUNDANCE
"GENEROSITY IS THE ANSWER TO FACE ABUNDANCE"
DR. BAK NGUYEN

Now that we've spent what seems to be a lifetime fighting the *elements* and the *Forces of Nature*, one must think that we've seen everything.

> "OUR PERSONAL LEGEND CAN ONLY BEGIN THE DAY THAT WE ARE OUT OF OUR QUEST OF IDENTITY."
> Dr. BAK NGUYEN

No matter on what quest you were fighting on, the *elements* and the *Forces of Nature* will dwell on you just the same. After finding some comfort in the arms of *Time* and then, rushing back on the field as if our life depended on the next fight, after walking through the forest and the *fog of Myopia*, after having stared *Truth* in the face and still walk tall with humility and grace, what else?

We are mounting our *beast* to destiny and to happiness, finding worth to our name. **Happiness**, is that the end? The reward of the warrior? Our fights and evolution brought us to new horizons and new heights. As our Nature is finally revealed and accepted, we are gaining in *Confidence* and *Strength* to grow into the *Momentum of Destiny*. Wins are accumulating not as ambitions but more as **consequences of our actions**.

People will join the victorious. Some will wait for us to fall and say: "I knew it!" They will even march on your corpse to prove their superiority. Until you wake up from death and look down on them. They aren't worth it...

The *Haters* will resent you all their lives. Eventually, they will simply avoid you. There are also the *cheerleaders*. They will acclaim and love you at first sight! You will never know what they really hold in their hearts since you cannot pin down what and why there are saying what they say.

From the *Haters*, at least, you know for a fact that their jealousy was so strong that they couldn't hold themselves silent, they had to burst out and criticize. They said out loud what they are: weak minds, fearful or victims of past failures from which they never recovered. What they are saying with their insults is the envy of your status as a *Force of Nature*. They are avoiding you eventually because Truth is taking over your presence to stare in their sad eyes.

The *cheerleaders*, they are doing so out of greed, not respect. They too, are noticing your wins and strengths, and they want in. They are feeding on you. They will eat as much as they can. Do not get too close, you might lose an arm.

And then, there's the Public, those undecided observing us and waiting to make up their minds. Depending on how we will react to both the *Cheerleaders* and the *Haters*, they will be siding eventually. They are holding the balance of power.

> **"LIFE IS ABOUT HAPPINESS. AND HAPPINESS IS ABOUT WORTH!"**
> Dr. BAK NGUYEN

As the public will join eventually your side, your *Momentum* will have reached a whole new level. Your status as a *Force of Nature* is no opinion anymore, it is a reality to be dealt with. With the favour of the crowd and the accumulation of glory and wealth, you will feel invincible. *Time* will whisper in your ear to marry her so this might last forever...

Life, your loyal spouse, is looking at you from the distance, leaving you to your glory. She is proud, she is happy and yet, silent and discreet. You have evolved and went to great lengths.

When you look at *Truth*, you are starting to like what you see from the glare of its eyes. So you embrace it. The joy, the glory, the victories, the popularity. You have just share the bed with *Abundance*, the prize of Nature.

If you thought that *Time* was *Aphrodite*, think again! *Abundance* is. She is kind and beautiful. She is the little cousin of *Life*. *Abundance* reassures you that within her arms, even *Life* will join you in your new destiny. Young, caring, voluptuous, nothing seems to resist her. She is not asking for anything in return. *Abundance* only requires you to be happy! So you drink from her lips, your victory and happiness.

But is this the end? Within the celebrations, a part of you will raise the question. Just like Hercules and Alexander the Great all felt, this cannot be it! As *Abundance* is everything you ever wished from Life, if you feed on this love for too long, you'll grow fat, lose your *momentum* and the worth you've built. *Inertia* will have won the last battle.

As much as I enjoy bedding with *Abundance*, my *Fear of God* is reminding me to take the road again. I will enjoy those moments of pleasure and joy, I'll be thankful, and I will have to go on, this time, knowing that I've reached happiness and I am looking beyond! This will be a great ending for a hero's myth.

Take leverage! That's who I am. I want it all! I don't want to march pass happiness if this is happiness. I don't want to miss out on what's beyond either since I will have to face God eventually. Even from the eyes of *Truth*, I am not sure where I stand anymore... things never seem so real and enchanting!

Abundance, oh my love for *Abundance*. What should I do **to be Abundance**, not just bed with her as a beneficiary? That question and the *fear of God* helped me to get back on my feet.

> **"GENEROSITY IS THE ANSWER TO FACE ABUNDANCE."**
> Dr. BAK NGUYEN

If I provide for *Abundance*, I will grow even taller, not fat but tall! And she will not feel rejected nor insulted, since I'll be joining her vibe, by her side, not just in her bed. I am a *Force of Nature*, I shall act as one. The day I embraced **Generosity**, that day, I grew to fit my destiny, fully.

> **"SHARING IS THE ONLY WAY TO GROW."**
> Dr. BAK NGUYEN

If you can grow from the bed of *Abundance* to keep your worth and name, you have joined the *Forces* of this world. You are proving that Humanity is more than apes looking to reproduce and differentiate. That's why I am fighting to raise the average instead of trying to beat it. From *Abundance*, I wake up and sleep every night looking to share the feeling and the vision with others.

She and her entourage will disagree with me, saying that *Abundance* is reserved for those who earn their way in. So I recognize *Two Faces* trying to make its way back into the game: to create scarcity over Abundance! What kind of mind trick is that? Neither *Inertia* nor *Two Faces* will win this one. I know better, I am generous and I fear God!

> "TO KEEP EVOLVING, COMFORT ZONES ARE OASIS TO REPLENISH AT, THEN, THE JOURNEY CONTINUES."
> Dr. BAK NGUYEN

If *Abundance* can follow me where I go, I will welcome the company. But I won't slow down to accommodate her nor her entourage. If they want me, it is for them to adapt their pace, not the other way around.

I will be providing and I will be happy. If she is not, I will keep happy memories of her and will move on, knowing that our paths will cross again. She will miss me as I never completely gave into her and her charms!

I am a *Force of Nature* by birthright, by choice, by freedom. I am generous and I fear God!

This is **FORCES OF NATURE**. Welcome to the Alphas.

ALL MY CHALLENGES WERE THE BIGGEST AS I FACED THEM AND VAGUE SOUVENIRS AS I MOVED ON

Dr. BAK NGUYEN

CONCLUSION - LIFE, DEATH
"ALL AWAKENINGS ARE BRUTAL"
DR. BAK NGUYEN

Now that we have passed happiness, that we have convinced *Abundance* to pack and to follow us in campaign, to keep pushing towards our destiny, most of the *Forces of Nature* have become elements of our entourage.

You see, they were always there as we were born, but we didn't notice them. Then, as we grew, we met each of them, face to face. They gained in importance and stature in our perception.

The unknown will empower each shadow to make it seems even bigger. And a shadow usually can make things appear way bigger than they really are. This is why, the first time we faced a *Force of Nature*, it is always intimidating and powerful. Powerful, it is and will remain. Intimidating, it depends.

> "INTIMIDATION IS NOT THE RECOGNITION OF THE STRENGTH OF ONE BUT RATHER THE LITTLENESS OF THE OTHER."
> Dr. BAK NGUYEN

This key helped me throughout my life, every time I faced a *Force of Nature*. Using that thinking, I forced myself to grow and to face each element, looking them in the eye, not as a daring exercise, but as a respectful bow. Respect from both ways.

Inertia was the first Mountain I had to climb. As high and steep as it was, today it serves as a reference point on my horizon. I have grown used to its presence. Even within the arms of *Abundance*, *Inertia* was the one reminding me that I was losing my sight as the mountain got closer and disappeared from my horizon. I've learnt my lesson, each day, I looked back to see:

> "IF THE SUN SETS BEHIND THE MOUNTAIN OF INERTIA, I KNOW THAT I AM WALKING IN THE RIGHT DIRECTION."
> Dr. BAK NGUYEN

Then, *Myopia*, that forest is miles behind. But if I let the joy and the magic of *Abundance* resonate for too long, the hand of *Myopia* will cover my eyes once more. Actually, every morning I wake up, I can still feel the oil of its hand covering my eyes. That is why everything looks blurry for the first few minutes of each day. I know that it will come back later in the night to check on me.

> "MYOPIA HAS ALWAYS BEEN THERE, IT HAS ALWAYS CARED. IF THE SIGHT IS BLURRY, ONE JUST NEEDS TO CHOOSE TO CLEAR HIS EYES FROM THE OIL."
> Dr. BAK NGUYEN

Knowing so, I am walking tall and confident knowing that each time *Myopia* is meeting me in the day, I just need to wake up. I do so swiftly and without hesitation since I know I will see it later at night... all in due and good time. Understanding *Myopia* revealed to me why most people are so mean and aggressive towards each other and even towards themselves... They are **sleepwalking**.

Don't stand on the way of a **sleepwalker**. He obeys Nature, and while under the influence of *Myopia*, he has its power to keep his state undisturbed, the power of a *Force of Nature*. Ever heard the saying to never wake a **sleepwalker**? If you must awake someone, do it so the first thing he will see is the sun and Life. But not too much light. And then, give him time to adjust.

> "ALL AWAKENINGS ARE BRUTAL. WITH TIME, WE ARE SIMPLY EXPECTING ITS EFFECTS."
> Dr. BAK NGUYEN

And then, we met with *Time*, the lover, the mistress. *Time* is one Force with whom we all share *a love and hate* relationship. It's always a matter of who's in control, of who's on top. Fighting with her, bedding her and then, being violently kicked to chase her back is the dance of seduction intended with her.

> "NO ONE CAN ESCAPE TIME. NO ONE CAN REALLY MASTER TIME.
> ONE CAN ONLY LEVERAGE TIME."
> Dr. BAK NGUYEN

So I made my peace with her. I keep seducing her and being kind to her. I also keep running my course to have her chasing me. I know that just like *Myopia*, she will be ahead of me, waiting even if I beat her racing.

She was cheering for me as I started and will embrace me as I arrive. Isn't that support? And the sex will be good as I will be on top. Only to change position to enjoy all that *Life* has to offer. It's not about winning but accepting first and then, leveraging.

Today, I know that *Time* is never too far away, even if she is showing no sign of her presence for a little while. I have please myself to say that I beat her in the race for a little longer. If I am not too cocky about it, her embrace ahead will be one of satisfaction instead of one of pride. The sex will be good either way, I just have my preference.

And then, there is *Truth*, the cold heart son of a bitch which will cast everything with its neon sight. It is surely a mood killer. It will eventually come to diminish as we gain its respect. Can you see, amongst the *Forces of Nature*, only we, are proud creatures? They are not.

Every time we saw pride it was because we were seeing them from the *reflection of our shield*. And every time we do so, the rust sets in and we are condemned to polish it once more.

I grew lazy and I have grown to leave the *shield* at the door. When I met with *Truth*, I came in offering tea. In the beginning, I showed up at its cold courtroom, bone-chilling cold. Today, I welcome the encounter but as I grew busy, sometimes it is *Truth* that comes to visit. For as long as we are just catching up with *Tea*, I am good.

> "I USE THE LIGHT OF TRUTH TO MAKE SURE THAT
> I AM POLISHING MYSELF AND NOT MY SHIELD."
> Dr. BAK NGUYEN

The work is even harder but since the rust is not settling back as soon as I look at it, I prefer this way. You see, I hate to do the same thing twice. I am done polishing my *shield of Pride* since it is a never-ending task with no chance for advancement. Furthermore, as I am pushing my journey forward, I know that eventually, I will have to present myself before God.

I also know that *Truth* will be the opposing counsel. The shield will be of little protection there. If there is one thing I will have to discard from Life is that *shield* that I left behind, somewhere. If that was an object of value, so be it, I will stand the trial. But I will have so much more to show for my defence.

All that I treasure are shinier and sharper as I use them, more and more. Just like a musical instrument will sound better the more it is played. My soul sings the same tune.

I learnt to discard or, at least, not to hold dear, everything that doesn't answer to the same standards. If they are getting rotten as I take them from the glass display, they should remain there, on display. So should be my *shield*... and I feel that *Truth* is agreeing with me since it never brought it up... until now.

Two Faces is a trickster. It has a sense of humour difficult to grasp. It will always try to have the last word at the end of the day. Actually, its trick is to make us play the game so we lose focus.

On that, its none verbal gave it up! So I learnt to laugh from its jokes, genuinely. To laugh from irony is a twisted way to find happiness. Whoever talked about happiness? To laugh has nothing to do with being happy! Laughing release the tension created and accumulated. That's all. As we feel lighter, we feel happy.

> **"HAPPINESS ISN'T FROM THE LAUGH BUT THE LIFT OF THE WEIGHT."**
> Dr. BAK NGUYEN

So I learnt to move lightweight, as much as possible. Even with the presence of *Abundance* and her entourage following me now, I am moving forward unburdened. I only wear my *speed* and my *Confidence*.

That's how sexy I remain to each of my lovers. They will all catch up! To that, I will drink! And *Two Faces* will be drinking to that too! All it needed was a good laugh.

> **"WE HAVE COME TO KNOW EACH OTHER WELL ENOUGH TO LAUGH TOGETHER, NOT AT EACH OTHER..."**
> Dr. BAK NGUYEN

Emotions, they are the powers holding my secrets. As I learnt to respect myself and my *inner beast*, I am whole. I am mounting my *Tornado* every day. I am caring for it, feeding it, and listening to it.

Contrary to a lover, *Emotions* don't need much attention, just the space to spread their legs and wings and to give in to their natural instincts. I am a knight thanks to my emotions.

Just like most in life, respect and understanding were the keys to my successful relationship with *Emotions*.

About the **virus**? Well, I still need the antibodies from *Expectations* to keep my system neat and ready to adapt to everything. I am fuelling from my own ambitions and the expectations I live up to are the ones derived from my ambitions, nothing more. As I have learnt to ignore the burden of the past and its expectations, I have also learnt to not transfer them to my son.

I took upon myself to break the curse and dispose of the burden, for the love of my son. His life is for him to choose and to bear. I will be a source of inspiration, nothing more. But I grew my wings and my strengths battling the legacy.

If anything, it made me grow into the man that my son now looks up to. From his eyes, I can recognize the look of *Truth*, without the neon lights...

> "AMBITIONS, NOT EXPECTATIONS."
> Dr. BAK NGUYEN

And from the voluptuous love of *Abundance*, I am replenishing and grateful. Grateful to have a lover to please without having to hold back anything. To be the man of the relationship, I had **to grow Generous**.

If anything, that will be the shiniest thing I have to show for, in front of God. *Abundance* is following me, from her free will. Open and kind, she even made a place for the other loves of my life.

> "ABUNDANCE AND GENEROSITY ALLOWED ME TO PUT AN END TO HAVING TO CHOOSE."
> Dr. BAK NGUYEN

I want or I don't. I do or I don't. I have ceased torturing myself between two goods or two evils. I am not afraid to pass out on something that I do not feel. Only God I fear. That's how humble I must stay, humble in the eye of God, not of men.

> "HUMILITY IS TO ACCEPT WHAT WE ARE AND TO STOP PRETENDING."
> Dr. BAK NGUYEN

I stopped pretending a long time ago since the rust was settling in too quickly. I do project though. To some, it all sounds the same. Well, it is not since pretending is to hold a shield, trying to hide the void. **Projecting is to fill the void with beliefs from the future**. It's not a matter of wording, but of beliefs.

Are you confident enough to bet on yourself and believe in the future?

I took the long road to avoid coming home. But home I must go to eventually. Well, you see, no one is perfect and we all have our shame. What about the first and kindest *Force of Nature*, Nature itself?

The *Angel of Life* whom I have made my wife, doesn't she feels betrayed by my love and sex life? As I come back home, she holds the same smile and calmness. She is cooking and smiling at me as I enter.

She hasn't changed. Actually, she was there all along but faded in the crowd of *Abundance* or in the background of my journey. She knows everything, but still has the kindness to ask for my journey and my stories. I give into her love. She has the patience to listen to each detail of each story. There is so much to tell.

In between the stories, she sees as I remained fed and rest. I can feel the caresses in my hair as I am falling asleep telling her my journey. I do not know for how long I talked but that morning, I woke up without *Myopia*. The woman looking back at me was *Life* as I knew her, but she was somehow different. I could see her, completely, for the first time. She is **Life and Death all at once**.

Strangely enough, I do not feel any menace. Just the same love, the same warmth. They say that *Oedipus* married his mother. Have I done the same? Has everyone done the same? *Life* was always ahead and bigger than me.

Zeus married *Hera* to become king and then, went on to look for himself. I cannot believe that the journey that I thought so unique was following a pattern, the pattern of our kind, of heroes and myths.

« Will I die? » I asked *Death or Life*. « Sure », she responds in kind. « But not yet. You have still to become unique and to find your worth, your true worth. »

It is not for me to know when I will run out of time. Honestly, I do not care. I am grateful for my life, for my love, for my journey, and the ones ahead. I know that one day, my spirit will outgrow my body, and eventually, I will reach a cliff bigger than one that I can jump. It is not of my concern. I still have many roads until I reach that cliff. I have grown strong and wise enough to stand with the *Forces of Nature*.

I am one with myself, completely. I am one with Nature and at her service. **Generous** and **Abundant**, I will remain. I will continue to grow bigger and stronger to provide to *Abundance* and to feed my own *Generosity*. That's my worth, that's my life. And when the time comes, I know the kindness that will be welcoming me, from the same woman I've loved all my life.

> "TO ALL THE WOMEN IN MY LIFE, PAST, PRESENT, AND FUTURE, YOU ARE LIGHT AND LOVE ALL AT ONCE."
> Dr. BAK NGUYEN

For you, I must grow and do you honour. May you be more difficult and demanding than God and you will have loved me with all your heart. I love you all.

And this concludes the Odysseus of the *Forces of Nature*. As I first started this journey, I did not know where it would lead. Sharing with you my challenges and giving them names and purpose made them universal, almost mythological.

Looking back at the journey, I must say that, as I am coming out from my trance writing, I am discovering the words and the chapters, just like you, for the first time.

May it helped you to make sense of your journey, of your scars, of your fresh wounds. You can't change the past, no one can. You can move on, stronger and wiser, or you can move on, diminished and handicapped. I am not sure that it is a choice, more a mindset and some luck.

In this kind of situation, one thing helps: to simulate the events without emotional involvement. This is what this journey was, a way for you to experience the journey, feelings, and sensations without facing your own demons. You faced mine instead.

And then, as you were ease-in, the mythology took over, blurring the faces and names of my personal story to make them into mirrors. The *demons*, *angels*, and *Forces of Nature* are the same, playing the same role, only, it will be for you to cast their faces and names.

You can't run from your own legend. You can't prepare for itself forever either. You experienced mine. As you recognize the horizon and the actors, face yours with confidence. Not the confidence that you know what is ahead, but with the confidence that others have walked similar journeys before.

Find strength in their legends. If not inspiration, at least, enough light to cast away the shadow of doubts. Now is your time, look up and beyond, and go find your name, your worth. Just remember that for as long as you face the sun, the shadow stays behind you.

This is **FORCES OF NATURE**. Welcome to the Alphas.

ALL MY CHALLENGES
WERE THE BIGGEST
AS I FACED THEM
AND VAGUE SOUVENIRS
AS I MOVED ON

Dr. BAK NGUYEN

ABOUT THE AUTHOR

From Canada, **Dr. BAK NGUYEN**, Nominee Ernst and Young Entrepreneur of the year, Grand Homage Lys DIVERSITY, LinkedIn & TownHall Achiever of the year and TOP 100 Doctors 2021. Dr Bak is a cosmetic dentist, CEO and founder of Mdex & Co. His company is revolutionizing the dental field. Speaker and motivator, he wrote 72 books over 36 months accumulating many world records (to be officialized). His books are covering:

- **ENTREPRENEURSHIP**
- **LEADERSHIP**
- **QUEST OF IDENTITY**
- **DENTISTRY AND MEDICINE**
- **PARENTING**
- **CHILDREN BOOKS**
- **PHILOSOPHY**

In 2003, he founded Mdex, a dental company upon which in 2018, he launched the most ambitious private endeavour to reform the dental industry, Canada wide. Philosopher, he has close to his heart the quest of happiness of the people surrounding him, patients and colleagues alike. In 2020, he launched an International collaborative initiative named **THE ALPHAS** to share knowledge and for Entrepreneurs and Doctors to thrive through the Greatest Pandemic and Economic depression of our time.

In 2016, he co-found with Tranie Vo, Emotive World Incorporated, a tech research company to use technology to empower happiness and sharing. U.A.X. the ultimate audio experience is the landmark project on which the team is advancing, utilizing the technics of the movie industry and the advancement in ARTIFICIAL INTELLIGENCE to save the book industry and to upgrade the continuing education space.

These projects have allowed Dr Nguyen to attract interests from the international and diplomatic community and he is now the center of a global discussion in the wellbeing and the future of the health profession. It is in that matter that he shares his thoughts and encourages the health community to share their own stories.

"It's not worth it go through it alone! Together, we stand, alone, we fall."

Motivational speaker and serial entrepreneur, philosopher and author, from his own words, Dr Nguyen describes himself as a dentist by circumstances, an entrepreneur by nature and a communicator by passion.

He also holds recognitions from the Canadian Parliament and the Canadian Senate.

www.DrBakNguyen.com

AMAZON - BARNES & NOBLE - APPLE BOOKS - KINDLE
SPOTIFY - APPLE MUSIC

ULTIMATE AUDIO EXPERIENCE

A new way to learn and enjoy Audiobooks. Made to be entertaining while keeping the self-educational value of a book, UAX will appeal to both auditive and visual people. UAX is the blockbuster of the Audiobooks.

UAX will cover most of Dr Bak's books, and is now negotiating to bring more authors and more titles to the UAX concept. Now streaming on Spotify, Apple Music and available for download on all major music platforms. Give it a try today!

AMAZON - BARNES & NOBLE - APPLE BOOKS - KINDLE
SPOTIFY - APPLE MUSIC

COMBO
PAPERBACK/AUDIOBOOK
ACTIVATION

Please register your book to receive the link to your audiobook version. Register at: https://drbaknguyen.com/forces-of-nature-registry

Your license of the audiobook allows you to share with up to 3 peoples the audiobook contained at this link. Book published by Dr. Bak publishing company. Audiobook produced by Emotive World Inc. Copyright 2021, All right reserved.

FROM THE SAME AUTHOR
Dr Bak Nguyen

www.DrBakNguyen.com

MAJOR LEAGUES' ACCESS

FACTEUR HUMAIN 032
LE LEADERSHIP DU SUCCÈS
par Dr. BAK NGUYEN & CHRISTIAN TRUDEAU

ehappyPedia 037
THE RISE OF THE UNICORN
BY Dr. BAK NGUYEN & Dr. JEAN DE SERRES

CHAMPION MINDSET 038
LEARNING TO WIN
BY Dr. BAK NGUYEN & CHRISTOPHE MULUMBA

BRANDING DrBAK 039
BALANCING STRATEGY AND EMOTIONS
BY Dr. BAK NGUYEN

THE RISE OF THE UNICORN 2 076
eHappyPedia
BY Dr BAK NGUYEN & Dr JEAN DE SERRES

002 **La Symphonie des Sens**
ENTREPREUNARIAT
par Dr. BAK NGUYEN

006 **Industries Disruptors**
BY Dr .BAK NGUYEN

007 **Changing the World from a dental chair**
BY Dr. BAK NGUYEN

008 **The Power Behind the Alpha**
BY TRANIE VO & Dr. BAK NGUYEN

035 **SELFMADE**
GRATITUDE AND HUMILITY
BY Dr. BAK NGUYEN

072 **THE U.A.X. STORY**
THE ULTIMATE AUDIO EXPERIENCE
BY Dr. BAK NGUYEN

BUSINESS

SYMPHONY OF SKILLS 001
BY Dr. BAK NGUYEN

CHILDREN'S BOOK
with William Bak

The Trilogy of Legends

THE LEGEND OF THE CHICKEN HEART 016
LA LÉGENDE DU COEUR DE POULET 017
BY Dr. BAK NGUYEN & WILLIAM BAK

THE LEGEND OF THE LION HEART 018
LA LÉGENDE DU COEUR DE LION 019
BY Dr. BAK NGUYEN & WILLIAM BAK

THE LEGEND OF THE DRAGON HEART 020
LA LÉGENDE DU COEUR DE DRAGON 021
BY Dr. BAK NGUYEN & WILLIAM BAK

WE ARE ALL DRAGONS 022
NOUS TOUS, DRAGONS 023
BY Dr. BAK NGUYEN & WILLIAM BAK

THE 9 SECRETS OF THE SMART CHICKEN 025
LES 9 SECRETS DU POULET INTELLIGENT 026
BY Dr. BAK NGUYEN & WILLIAM BAK

THE SECRET OF THE FAST CHICKEN 027
LE SECRETS DU POULET RAPIDE 028
BY Dr. BAK NGUYEN & WILLIAM BAK

THE LEGEND OF THE SUPER CHICKEN 029
LA LÉGENDE DU SUPER POULET 030
BY Dr. BAK NGUYEN & WILLIAM BAK

031 **THE STORY OF THE CHICKEN SHIT**
032 **L'HISTOIRE DU CACA DE POULET**
BY Dr. BAK NGUYEN & WILLIAM BAK

033 **WHY CHICKEN CAN'T DREAM?**
034 **POURQUOI LES POULETS NE RÊVENT PAS?**
BY Dr. BAK NGUYEN & WILLIAM BAK

057 **THE STORY OF THE CHICKEN NUGGET**
083 **HISTOIRE DE POULET: LA PÉPITE**
BY Dr. BAK NGUYEN & WILLIAM BAK

082 **CHICKEN FOREVER**
084 **POULET POUR TOUJOURS**
BY Dr. BAK NGUYEN & WILLIAM BAK

THE SPIES AND ALIENS COLLECTION

077 **THE VACCINE**
079 **LE VACCIN**
077B **LA VACUNA**
BY Dr BAK NGUYEN & WILLIAM BAK
TRANSLATION BY BRENDA GARCIA

DENTISTRY

PROFESSION HEALTH - TOME ONE 005
THE UNCONVENTIONAL
QUEST OF HAPPINESS
BY Dr. BAK NGUYEN, Dr. MIRJANA SINDOLIC,
Dr. ROBERT DURAND AND COLLABORATORS

HOW TO NOT FAIL AS A DENTIST 046
BY Dr. BAK NGUYEN

SUCCESS IS A CHOICE 060
BLUEPRINTS FOR HEALTH
PROFESSIONALS
BY Dr. BAK NGUYEN

RELEVANCY - TOME TWO 064
REINVENTING OURSELVES TO SURVIVE
BY Dr. BAK NGUYEN & Dr. PAUL OUELLETTE AND
COLLABORATORS

MIDAS TOUCH 065
POST-COVID DENTISTRY
BY Dr. BAK NGUYEN, Dr. JULIO REYNAFARJE AND
Dr. PAUL OUELLETTE

THE POWER OF DR 066
THE MODERN TITLE OF NOBILITY
BY Dr. BAK NGUYEN, Dr. PAVEL KRASTEV AND
COLLABORATORS

QUEST OF IDENTITY

004 **IDENTITY**
THE ANTHOLOGY OF QUESTS
BY Dr. BAK NGUYEN

011 **HYBRID**
THE MODERN QUEST OF IDENTITY
BY Dr. BAK NGUYEN

015 **FORCES OF NATURE**
FORGING THE CHARACTER
OF WINNERS
BY Dr. BAK NGUYEN

LIFESTYLE

045 **HORIZON, BUILDING UP THE VISION**
VOLUME ONE
BY Dr. BAK NGUYEN

047- **HORIZON, ON THE FOOTSTEPS
OF TITANS**
VOLUME TWO
BY Dr. BAK NGUYEN

068- **HORIZON, DREAMING OF TRAVELING**
VOLUME THREE
BY Dr. BAK NGUYEN

MILLION DOLLAR MINDSET

MOMENTUM TRANSFER 009
BY Dr. BAK NGUYEN & Coach DINO MASSON

LEVERAGE 014
COMMUNICATION INTO SUCCESS
BY Dr. BAK NGUYEN AND COLLABORATORS

**HOW TO WRITE A BOOK
IN 30 DAYS** 040
BY Dr. BAK NGUYEN

POWER 042
EMOTIONAL INTELLIGENCE
BY Dr. BAK NGUYEN

**HOW TO WRITE A
SUCCESSFUL BUSINESS PLAN** 048
BY Dr BAK NGUYEN & ROUBA SAKR

MINDSET ARMORY 049
BY Dr. BAK NGUYEN

**MASTERMIND, 7 WAYS
INTO THE BIG LEAGUE** 052
BY Dr. BAK NGUYEN & JONAS DIOP

PLAYBOOK INTRODUCTION 055
BY Dr. BAK NGUYEN

PLAYBOOK INTRODUCTION 2 056
BY Dr. BAK NGUYEN

062 **RISING**
TO WIN MORE THAN YOU
ARE AFRAID TO LOSE
BY Dr. BAK NGUYEN

067 **TORNADO**
FORCE OF CHANGE
BY Dr. BAK NGUYEN

071 **BOOTCAMP**
BOOKS TO REWRITE MINDSETS
INTO WINNING STATES OF MIND
BY Dr. BAK NGUYEN

PARENTING

024 **THE BOOK OF LEGENDS**
BY Dr. BAK NGUYEN & WILLIAM BAK

041 **THE BOOK OF LEGENDS 2**
BY Dr. BAK NGUYEN & WILLIAM BAK

051 **THE BOOK OF LEGENDS 3**
THE END OF THE INNOCENCE AGE
BY Dr. BAK NGUYEN & WILLIAM BAK

PERSONAL GROWTH

REBOOT 012
MIDLIFE CRISIS
BY Dr. BAK NGUYEN

HUMILITY FOR SUCCESS 050
BALANCING STRATEGY AND EMOTIONS
BY Dr. BAK NGUYEN

THE ENERGY FORMULA 053
BY Dr. BAK NGUYEN

AMONGST THE ALPHA 058
BY Dr. BAK NGUYEN & COLLABORATORS

AMONGST THE ALPHA vol.2 059
ON THE OTHER SIDE
BY Dr. BAK NGUYEN & COLLABORATORS

THE 90 DAYS CHALLENGE 061
BY Dr. BAK NGUYEN

EMPOWERMENT 069
BY Dr BAK NGUYEN

THE MODERN WOMAN 070
TO HAVE IT HAVE WITH NO SACRIFICE
BY Dr. BAK NGUYEN & Dr. EMILY LETRAN

ALPHA LADDERS 075
CAPTAIN OF YOUR DESTINY
BY Dr BAK NGUYEN & JONAS DIOP

PHILOSOPHY

003 **LEADERSHIP**
PANDORA'S BOX
BY Dr. BAK NGUYEN

043 **KRYPTO**
TO SAVE THE WORLD
BY Dr. BAK NGUYEN & ILYAS BAKOUCH

SOCIETY

013 **LE RÊVE CANADIEN**
D'IMMIGRANT À MILLIONNAIRE
par DR BAK NGUYEN

054 **CHOC**
LE JARDIN D'EDITH
par DR BAK NGUYEN

063 **AFTERMATH**
BUSINESS AFTER THE GREAT PAUSE
BY Dr BAK NGUYEN & Dr ERIC LACOSTE

073 **TOUCHSTONE**
LEVERAGING TODAY'S P
SYCHOLOGICAL SMOG
BY Dr BAK NGUYEN & Dr KEN SEROTA

074 **COVIDCONOMICS**
THE GENERATION AHEAD
BY Dr BAK NGUYEN & COLLABORATORS

ALPHA LADDERS 2 081
SHAPING LEADERS AND ACHIEVERS
BY Dr BAK NGUYEN & BRENDA GARCIA

THE POWER OF YES 010
VOLUME ONE: IMPACT
BY Dr BAK NGUYEN

THE POWER OF YES 2 036
VOLUME TWO: SHAPELESS
BY Dr BAK NGUYEN

THE POWER OF YES 3 039
VOLUME THREE: LIMITLESS
BY Dr BAK NGUYEN

THE POWER OF YES 4 085
VOLUME FOUR: PURPOSE
BY Dr BAK NGUYEN

THE POWER OF YES 5 086
VOLUME FIVE: ALPHA
BY Dr BAK NGUYEN

THE POWER OF YES 6 087
VOLUME SIX: PERSPECTIVE
BY Dr BAK NGUYEN

TITLES AVAILABLE AT

www.DrBakNguyen.com

AMAZON - BARNES & NOBLE - APPLE BOOKS - KINDLE
SPOTIFY - APPLE MUSIC

TITLES AVAILABLE AT
www.DrBakNguyen.com

AMAZON - BARNES & NOBLE - APPLE BOOKS - KINDLE
SPOTIFY - APPLE MUSIC

www.ingramcontent.com/pod-product-compliance
Lightning Source LLC
Chambersburg PA
CBHW071504150426
43191CB00009B/1410